CITYSPOTS
AMSTERDAM

Mike Gerrard

Thomas Cook

GW00497288

Written by Mike Gerrard
Updated by Dara Colwell

Published by Thomas Cook Publishing
A division of Thomas Cook Tour Operations Limited
Company registration No: 1450464 England
The Thomas Cook Business Park, 9 Coningsby Road
Peterborough PE3 8SB, United Kingdom
Email: books@thomascook.com, Tel: +44 (0)1733 416477
www.thomascookpublishing.com

Produced by The Content Works Ltd
Aston Court, Kingsmead Business Park, Frederick Place
High Wycombe, Bucks HP11 1LA
www.thecontentworks.com

Series design based on an original concept by Studio 183 Limited

ISBN: 978-1-84157-916-0

First edition © 2006 Thomas Cook Publishing
This second edition © 2008 Thomas Cook Publishing
Text © Thomas Cook Publishing
Maps © Thomas Cook Publishing/PCGraphics (UK) Limited
Transport map © Communicarta Limited

Series Editor: Kelly Anne Pipes
Project Editor: Linda Bass
Production: Steven Collins

Printed and bound in Spain by GraphyCems

Cover photography (House with shutters) © Terry Williams/Getty Images

CONTENTS

SYMBOLS KEY

The following symbols are used throughout this book:

ⓐ address ☎ telephone 🅕 fax 🅦 website address 🅔 email
🅛 opening times 🅝 public transport connections

The following symbols are used on the maps:

- ℹ️ information office
- ✈ airport
- ➕ hospital
- 🛡 police station
- 🚌 bus station
- 🚆 railway station
- Ⓜ metro
- ✝ cathedral
- ❶ numbers denote featured cafés & restaurants

- ▮ points of interest
- O city
- O large town
- o small town
- ═ motorway
- — main road
- — minor road
- — railway

Hotels and restaurants are graded by approximate price as follows:
£ budget price ££ mid-range price £££ expensive

▶ *Introducing Amsterdam, the national monument*

Introduction

A living, breathing city that has always attracted outsiders – be they tourists, philosophers, hippies or immigrants – Amsterdam has great and enduring charm. Its population, currently around a million, is small compared to that of most capital cities but its people are as cosmopolitan and forward-thinking as anywhere in the world.

The correct name for the country of which Amsterdam is the capital is the Netherlands. Although people often call it Holland, they are mistakenly referring to the actual province, North Holland, in which the city is located.

What makes the city unique is a combination of both its beauty and its people. Amsterdam's canals, lined with lofty buildings, criss-crossed by simple little bridges and traversed by hundreds of cyclists, are something truly special. They may not be as grand as those of Venice, but you can enjoy them on a much more human scale.

The Dutch people have always been known for their tolerance and Amsterdam is a city in which you can immediately relax, whoever you are and whatever you want to do.

Some people who have never smoked in their lives come to Amsterdam to take a puff in the famous cannabis cafés or coffeeshops. A proposed ban on smoking in public places has repeatedly threatened this most renowned of Amsterdam's institutions, but it appears now that the ban, when it comes in, will only apply to the small area of the shop where marijuana is actually sold. The rest of the café can be as smoky and as atmospheric as it was in the 1960s.

Others who would never dream of visiting a prostitute head straight for the city's infamous red light district, whose bright lights and extravagant displays attract curiosity seekers as well as some rather more undesirable elements.

There's far more to Amsterdam than notorious pursuits. It has two of the finest art museums in the world, the Rijksmuseum and the Van Gogh Museum, not to mention Rembrandt's original house and studio. The Anne Frank House, where the Frank family hid from the Nazis during World War II, makes for a powerful and sobering visit.

Above and beyond its attractions, though, Amsterdam is about its atmosphere, its bars and brown cafés, its cheap and cheerful Indonesian restaurants, street markets, quirky shops and friendly locals.

MUSHROOMS
HERbS
SEEDS
BOOKS
GIFTS
iNTERNET
E-ZZZZZ
OXYGEN

○ *You'll find more than coffee in a coffeeshop*

When to go

There's no doubt that Amsterdam is a summer city, even though
the weather may not always be as summery as you might like.
Most people visit from April to October, with the biggest influx
during the July and August school holidays. To catch the sun and
avoid the crowds, try to visit Amsterdam in spring or autumn.
Winter can also be atmospheric, and it's a great place to come
for Christmas shopping if you remember to wrap up warm.

SEASONS & CLIMATE

Summers are generally mild and winters can be cold and damp.
It seldom gets very hot in the city, even in the height of summer,
although it can be rather sticky if it does. It's unlikely the canals
will freeze again in winter, as they did in 1998, but sometimes it
feels like they should. It can rain at any time of year. What's more,
if the temperature drops the canals can add an extra chill, so pack
with that in mind. But be prepared for anything, all year round –
pocket-sized umbrellas and extra layers are the key.

ANNUAL EVENTS

If you don't mind a crowd, book early for the best party in town, the
Queen's official birthday at the end of April. The city is packed with
visitors of all nationalities, mostly dressed in the national colour of
orange, and the event is like an extraordinary all-day flea market. August
is also the time for crowds and celebrations, including the unique
Gay Pride Boat Parade and the excellent music and theatre festivals.

For up-to-date information on current festivals and events, call the
tourist office (see page 152) or check ⓦ www.amsterdam.info/events
or ⓦ www.iamsterdam.com

February
Carnival takes place every year in the Brabant region, roughly two hours from Amsterdam. The weather doesn't quite rival Rio's, but there is a buzz about the place and a lot of action on the streets.

🔺 *National Windmill Day in May sees windmills in action countrywide*

April & May

National Museum Week Free or reduced entry to the country's great art museums. There are also special events and exhibitions. Usually around the second weekend of April.

Koninginnedag (Queen's official birthday) The biggest and best celebration in Amsterdam, held on 30 April. Book accommodation in advance.

National Windmill Day Amsterdam's windmills are opened up and the sails set working. Other windmills all over the country are also set working. What could be more Dutch than this? The event usually takes place on the second Saturday in May.

August

Amsterdam Pride Gay Pride celebration at the start of August, including a unique Gay Pride Boat Parade on the canals. The streets are packed and you should expect to see some extravagant outfits and outrageous behaviour. Ⓦ www.amsterdamgaypride.nl

De Parade Travelling theatre festival, offering a wonderful mix of art, theatre, music and food. The festival has been going strong for 15 years. Shows last anything from five minutes to an hour – just show up and buy tickets on the festival grounds. Ⓦ www.deparade.nl

Grachtenfestival (Canal festival) takes place the second week in August. Each year sees a different theme and internationally renowned musicians performing along canals and the river. Ⓦ www.grachtenfestival.nl

September

Open Monumentendag (Open Monuments Day) usually takes place on the second Saturday in September. Many private historical buildings in the city throw open their doors to the public, often free

of charge, for an exclusive visit. ⓦ www.openmonumentendag.nl
Robodock A spectacularly inventive multimedia festival held within
an industrial backdrop, Robodok brings together international
designers, architects, theatrical performers, musicians and robots.
Usually held mid-September. ⓦ www.robodock.org

November–January
Sinterklaas Parade Santa Claus arrives by boat at Centraal Station
on the third Saturday in November, then parades through the
streets to Dam Square. His black-faced helpers, known as Zwarte
Piet (Black Peter), throw sweets to the children in the crowds.
ⓦ www.stnicholascenter.org
New Year One of Europe's biggest celebrations in one of its most
compact cities. Beware the local custom of throwing fireworks.

PUBLIC HOLIDAYS
New Year's Day 1 January
Good Friday 21 March 2008, 10 April 2009, 2 April 2010
Easter Sunday & Monday 23 & 24 March 2008, 12 & 13 April 2009,
4 & 5 April 2010
Koninginnedag (Queen's birthday) 30 April
Ascension Day 1 May 2008, 21 May 2009, 13 May 2010
Pentecost Sunday & Monday 11 & 12 May 2008, 31 May &
1 June 2009, 23 & 24 May 2010
Christmas & Boxing Day 25 & 26 December

Businesses, including some shops and restaurants, are usually
closed on **Remembrance Day** (4 May) and **Liberation Day** (5 May).

The Heineken story

Although Heineken beer hasn't been made in Amsterdam since 1988, when the city brewery was closed and later turned into the Heineken Experience visitor attraction, it is part of the national consciousness. Amsterdammers drink an incredible 80,000 bottles of it every hour.

It was 1863 when Gerard Adriaan Heineken, a 22-year-old Dutch entrepreneur, bought the brewery that overlooks the Singelgracht canal in Amsterdam. The brewery had been going steady since 1592.

🔺 *Allow a couple of hours for a tour of the old Heineken brewery*

He changed its name from *De Hooiberg* (The Haystack) to his family name and began putting his time and energy into making Dutch beer into a huge export business. Ask for a beer in any continental European country now and you'll often be offered a choice of Heineken or Amstel, both Dutch brews. It's an impressive feat, considering brewing has always been more traditionally linked with countries such as Germany, Belgium and Great Britain.

Within five years of Heineken buying The Haystack, several other breweries had opened in the city. Heineken cleverly stayed ahead of the competition by buying bars and hotels, to ensure his brew had guaranteed outlets. In 1874 Heineken expanded to Rotterdam with a state-of-the-art brewery. Quality took precedence over price and word of mouth proved more successful than advertising, leading to a reputation for a consistently good brew. Soon Heineken was the biggest exporter of beer to Paris, which was developing rapidly as the most important city in Europe at the end of the 19th century. Throughout this time he kept it as his family business and it remains so to this day.

Ironically, it was Heineken's success that led to the original brewery in Amsterdam being closed in 1988. Production had expanded so much that it was increasingly difficult to get large delivery lorries through the narrow streets. The old shire horses delivering beer locally may have looked picturesque, but they couldn't quite manage to keep up with 80,000 bottles an hour, or the huge demand for exports. By 1989 Heineken had become the largest brewer in Europe, the second largest in the world and the biggest exporter of beer to the USA. The beer has won many international prizes over the years.

The Heineken Experience (see page 82), was opened in the former brewery in 2001, and is now one of the city's most popular attractions.

History

Amsterdam's name comes from the dam built by fishermen at the mouth of the Amstel river in the early 13th century. They built their homes on the top of small mounds and the fishing village of Amstelledamme was born.

In the 14th century the community flourished as a centre of trade and the first canals were dug. In 1602 the Dutch East India Company was founded. It became hugely successful through its spice trade with Asia and by the end of the 17th century Amsterdam was the biggest port in the world. Amsterdam's Canal Ring was built, in effect turning the city into a series of islands connected by bridges.

In 1806 Napoleon Bonaparte conquered the Netherlands and declared his brother Louis the new king. His reign didn't last. By 1813, the Dutch had regained their independence and William I his throne.

The discovery of diamond fields at the end of the 19th century in South Africa, then part of the Dutch empire, has made Amsterdam a world centre for diamond trading.

During World War I the Netherlands maintained its independence, but it was occupied by German forces from 1940–45 in World War II.

HERRING
Amsterdam owes its existence to herring. Fisherman had always trawled these waters for herring, but a permanent settlement only came into existence when they learned how to preserve the fish so that more could be brought ashore, processed and sold. The original settlement was actually in what is still the centre of Amsterdam life, Dam Square.

The turbulent 1960s saw Amsterdam gain a reputation as the radical heart of Europe for its tolerance towards soft drugs, its politically active youth and the widespread squatting caused by a housing shortage. Immigrants from Suriname, Turkey and Morocco started flocking to the city in the 1980s, attracted by a burgeoning service industry.

As the new century dawned, social problems such as ethnic and sexual discrimination increased and religious differences – half of the city's population has been born to non-Dutch parents – began to emerge. In 2001, gay marriage was legalised, though there was strong opposition from fundamentalist religious groups. In 2004, the murder of media celebrity Theo Van Gogh, killed by a young Moroccan radical, quickly proved that Amsterdam's famed multiculturalism and tolerance was facing a severe test. Things have calmed in recent years and the city continues to attract tourists for its beauty, architecture, canals and above all, progressive attitude.

● *Herring is still a popular snack in Amsterdam*

Lifestyle

One word describes the city's vibe: *gezellig*. It roughly translates as cosy, but signifies everything that makes Amsterdam and its people feel relaxed, comfortable, snug and happy. *Gezellig* is how Amsterdammers describe an evening spent in the company of friends and how they feel about making new friends. *Gezellig* is how you will feel in Amsterdam, in a warm bar on a cold night after a couple of drinks, with music in the background and easy conversation all around.

The Dutch are stylish, but unlike in many modern cities Amsterdammers are not overly style-conscious or neurotic. They are happy to travel around on bicycles and the most basic of bicycles at that. You are more likely to see an achingly beautiful young woman or a smartly suited businessman cycling by on a sit-up-and-beg

● *One of Amsterdam's many brown bars*

boneshaker than a designer bicycle. For Amsterdammers, the point is to get where they want to go.

This relaxed attitude and lifestyle links in with the city's famed reputation for tolerance. But don't be fooled. Tolerance has its rules and limits and Amsterdam is in no way anarchistic. You can smoke cannabis in some coffee houses, but you can't walk down the street puffing away brazenly. If you do, you'll find the police aren't quite so *gezellig* after all.

Prices are fairly reasonable in Amsterdam, too. The cost of living is about average for northern Europe, perhaps a touch cheaper than London or Paris, but not dramatically so. Hotels are expensive, so if you are on a budget try to visit at quieter times of the year or start searching early for a special deal. The good thing is that you won't be shelling out on taxis or public transport. Amsterdam is compact – and cosy – enough for you to stroll across it in less than an hour.

Culture

Amsterdam is one of the world's great art cities. Two men are, for the most part, responsible for this: Rembrandt and Van Gogh. Rembrandt was 25 when he came to Amsterdam in 1631. He lived there until his death in 1669 and you can visit his house and the studio in which he painted, the Museum Het Rembrandthuis (Rembrandt's House Museum) (see pages 70–1). Some of his major works are also on display in the Rijksmuseum (see pages 96–7).

Combine Rembrandt's work with the greatest Van Gogh collection in the world and that's reason enough for art lovers to visit Amsterdam. The Van Gogh Museum is one of the city's most visited attractions (see pages 98–9). The Stedelijk, Amsterdam's Modern Art Museum (see page 100) also houses unusual and provocative works by some of the world's great names.

If classical music and dance are more your cultural scene, then look out for what's on at the Concertgebouw (see page 96). The National Ballet and the Netherlands Opera regularly perform there and they both have a good reputation. The Royal Concertgebouw Orchestra, the Netherlands Philharmonic Orchestra and the Netherlands Chamber Orchestra are also based in the city. There are several other venues where you can find dance, drama and music being performed, ranging from stalwart classics to the more cutting-edge. Check posters and websites for what is on offer while you're here.

Amsterdam is a young, vibrant city and you'll find plenty of more modern and upbeat music around the city. Big-name bands often perform in Amsterdam as part of their European tours. The Paradiso

● *Rembrandt and Van Gogh dominate the city's cultural scene*

⬤ *The Van Gogh Museum is the city's top tourist attraction*

(see page 105) and the Amsterdam ArenA (see page 32) are two of the bigger venues, but in smaller halls and clubs throughout the city you'll find variations of rock, world music, folk, jazz and blues. Amsterdammers love music and musicians seem to love the city in return.

If you are interested in history and the fine arts, there are plenty of small museums, churches and other old buildings of architectural interest to keep you occupied. But whatever you do, don't miss out on the things that really make Amsterdam stand out: Van Gogh, Rembrandt, the infamous red light district and cannabis culture, the bars and brown cafés and finally its everyday life.

▶ *You can't get away from bikes and canals*

MAKING THE MOST OF
Amsterdam

Shopping

Thankfully, Amsterdam is not the neon-lit shopping capital of the world. Instead of designer names and department stores, the city offers individual shops and boutiques selling anything from clogs to condoms, Dutch cheese to diamonds and explosive liqueurs to non-alcoholic tipples. Many excellent specialist shops can be found

MARKETS

Other than jewellery shops, the best and certainly cheaper bargains are in the flea markets, which take place around the city throughout the week. One of the best and longest-running street markets is to the south in the De Pijp district. The Albert Cuypmarkt (see page 87) is also a colourful affair, with a few hundred stalls running between Ferdinand Bolstraat and Van Woustraat selling everything from cheap fashion and textiles to fresh vegetables. A visit to the Bloemenmarkt (Flower Market, see page 87) along the Singel canal near Muntplein will provide you with lots of colourful photos.

Foodies should head straight for the various busy food markets and in particular the cheese stalls. Everyone knows about Dutch cheeses such as Edam and Gouda, but you'll quickly discover that these are actually two of the blandest cheeses made in the country. They're produced mainly for export – the Dutch keep the tastier cheese for themselves. Spices however are anything but bland. Dutch links with Southeast Asia, especially Indonesia, mean that you'll find a variety of spices and unusual fruits on sale.

⬤ *There's more to Dutch cheese than Edam and Gouda*

along the *negen straatjes* (nine streets) running from the Singel canal to Prinsengracht.

If you're on the hunt for a diamond ring or other piece of jewellery, then you'll find prices competitive and the selection impressive. You can also take a free factory tour to learn a bit about what you're buying (see pages 80 and 92).

USEFUL SHOPPING PHRASES

How much is...?
Hoeveel kost (het)...?
Hoo-fay! kost (het)...?

Can I try this on?
Mag ik dit passen?
Makh ik dit passen?

I'm a size...
Ik heb maat...
Ik hep maat...

I'll take this one
Deze neem ik
Day-ze naym ik

Eating & drinking

Amsterdam is buzzing with great places to eat, with everything from cheap cafés to the finest gourmet cuisine. Much on offer is international – there are excellent Italian, Japanese, Chinese, Indian, African, American and Caribbean restaurants – but traditional cuisine from the Netherlands and other countries close by, such as Belgian, Flemish, Scandinavian and German, is also popular.

One international speciality you shouldn't miss is Indonesian food. There is a large Indonesian population in Amsterdam thanks to the close trading ties between the Netherlands and the East

BROWN BARS, COFFEESHOPS AND TASTING HOUSES

If you simply want a coffee, don't go to a coffeeshop, which is the term for shops that sell marijuana as well as the usual coffees, drinks and snacks. For the drug-free option, you need a café. If you're looking for a decent meal and not just a coffee, choose an *eetcafé*, which has a wider menu.

Brown bars and brown cafés are actually so-called because of the colour the walls become after years of people meeting there for a chat and a smoke. Brown bars serve more alcoholic drinks while brown cafés serve more soft drinks; both offer food of some kind.

Look out for the remaining few *proeflokalen* (tasting houses). These were originally created for the distillers producing the Dutch gin *jenever*, though independent tasting houses soon sprang up too. There are still a few left around the city if you are looking for a drop of something stronger.

🔺 *Al fresco dining on Nieuwmarkt*

Indies, and there are countless restaurants serving this tasty and spicy cooking. Try the *rijsttafel* (rice table), a selection of small beef and seafood dishes served with rice. It can be extremely filling, so save it for when you're really hungry.

◐ *Help the Amsterdammers get through some of that Heineken*

Indonesian restaurants are also good for non-meat dishes, although vegetarians should have no trouble in Amsterdam finding good food to eat. With its long association with alternative culture, vegetarianism has been around for many years. There are several vegetarian restaurants and most regular places offer vegetarian options.

Hotel breakfasts are usually continental and included in the price of the room. If you want orange juice you may have to ask for it, as it isn't always served automatically. The Dutch tend to eat early, so lunch begins about noon and dinner is served from 18.00 onwards.

PRICE CATEGORIES
Ratings are based on the rough cost of a three-course meal for one person, excluding drinks.
£ up to €20   ££ €20–€30   £££ over €30

Many restaurants start to wind down by 22.00, when last orders are taken. If you like to eat late, your choice will be somewhat limited and you should first check out opening hours.

Tipping is not a big part of Dutch culture. A service charge is usually included in the bill – simply round up to the nearest euro or leave any spare change if you have enjoyed particularly good service.

USEFUL DINING PHRASES

I'd like a table for (two) please
Graag een tafel voor (twee) personen
Khraakh an taa-fel for (tway) persoanen

Could I have the bill please?
De rekening alstublieft?
De ray-ken-ing als-too bleeft?

Waiter!
Ober!
Oaber!

Does it have meat in it?
Zitten er vlees in?
Zitten air vlees in?

Where are the toilets?
Waar is het toilet?
Vaar is het twa-let?

Entertainment & nightlife

You'll find it hard not to have fun in Amsterdam. Whatever you want to do, you can usually do it – and that includes a few things you can't do in too many other cities.

Amsterdam is beautiful by day but comes into its own after dark. The infamous red light district near Centraal Station might not be everyone's idea of a fun time, but it undeniably has its own kind of neon attraction and you shouldn't miss it.

The Leidseplein near the Jordaan district is the place where teenagers hang out in bars and cafés and is a lively place to go for fast food. A trendier area is Spuikwartier, around Spuistraat, packed with bars, clubs, restaurants and some of Amsterdam's best brown bars.

If Amsterdam is a party town any night of the year, it's double the fun when there's a festival going on. One of the biggest and best parties is the Queen's birthday on 30 April and the city's streets are heaving around that time. Throughout the year, particularly in summer, there are many music, theatre and film festivals.

For music, dance and drama performances of all sorts, Amsterdam can't be beaten. Weekly listings can be found in *Amsterdam Weekly*, the city's only English arts and entertainment newspaper. Make sure you look for flyers in bars and music shops advertising local clubs and special gigs.

You can buy tickets for many events in tourist information offices and travel agents. Bigger hotels will also book tickets for you. Alternatively, one of the biggest ticket agencies in the city is **AUB** (ⓐ Leidseplein 26, corner Marnixstraat ⓣ 020 621 1311 ⓦ www.amsterdamsuitburo.nl ⓛ 10.00–19.30 Mon–Sat,

---

◗ *A typical sign in the red light district*

12.00–19.30 Sun 🔵 Tram: 1, 2, 5, 6, 10, 17 to Leidseplein). You can book tickets on the AUB website before you leave home.

Cinemas often play big releases and American films in the original language, with Dutch subtitles. Films are occasionally dubbed in Dutch, though, so do check before buying a ticket.

Visitors looking for the gay and lesbian scene should have no trouble finding entertainment, as the city's long-established tolerance means that many gay clubs and areas have sprung up. Ask at the **COC Centre** (🅐 Rozenstraat 14 🕿 020 626 3087 🅦 www.cocamsterdam.nl 🔵 Tram: 13, 17; Bus: 170, 172 to Westermarkt) for information on the

gay scene. Or check out the **Pink Point of Presence**, Europe's only gay and lesbian information kiosk (ⓦ www.pinkpoint.org ⏰ 10.00–18.00 Ⓝ Tram: 13,17; Bus: 170, 172 to Westermarkt), located next to the **Homomonument**, the city's huge, phallic war memorial in Westermarkt.

One word of warning for those letting their hair down: the city's tolerance means that soft drugs are openly smoked in some nightclubs, but be aware that the buying and selling of drugs is still technically illegal.

◐ *The elegant Magere Brug at night*

Sport & relaxation

SPECTATOR SPORTS
American football The city's team are the Amsterdam Admirals, based at the Amsterdam ArenA. Details of fixtures can be obtained from the stadium. ❸ Arena Blvd 1 ❶ 020 311 1333 ⓦ www.amsterdamarena.nl ⓐ Metro: 50 to Bijlmer/ArenA; Bus: 29, 158, 174, 177, 178

Football City stars Ajax (ⓦ www.ajax.nl) play at the Amsterdam ArenA (see above). Home match or not, real fans will want to do the stadium tour.

PARTICIPATION
Bicycle rental Amsterdam and the bicycle were made for each other and there are plenty of bike rental places about the city. Try **MacBike**

⬤ Bikes: as plentiful as tulips

(ⓐ Visserplein 2 ⓣ 020 620 0985 ⓦ www.macbike.nl) and remember to take your passport.

Cycle tours Enjoy a guided cycle tour of the city or even further afield. Try **Mike's Bike Tours** (ⓐ Kerkstraat 134 ⓣ 020 622 7970 ⓦ www.mikesbikeamsterdam.com ⓝ Tram: 16, 24, 25 to Kerkstraat) or **Yellow Bike Tours** (ⓐ Nieuwzijds Kolk 29 ⓣ 020 620 6940 ⓦ www.yellowbike.nl ⓝ Five-min. walk from Centraal Station). These companies also offer one-day and longer bike rentals.

Rollerblading You can rent skates at the southern entrance to the Vondelpark on Amstelveenseweg. Every Friday night in summer thousands of skaters take a 14.5 km (9 mile) route through the city centre, leaving from the Filmmuseum in Vondelpark at 20.00. ⓦ www.fridaynightskate.com

RELAXATION
Blijburg aan Zee A man-made beach complete with beach restaurant. A mix of exotic and hippy, this is where trendy locals come to drink, eat tapas and listen to DJs spinning tracks. ⓐ Bert Haanstrakade 2004 ⓣ 020 416 0330 ⓦ www.blijburg.nl ⓝ Tram: 26

Sauna For some pampering, head for **Sauna Deco** (ⓐ Herengracht 115 ⓣ 020 623 8215 ⓦ www.saunadeco.nl ⓝ Tram: 1, 2, 5 to Magna Plaza/ Dam Square), with its art deco stained-glass windows, steam baths, saunas and cold-water swimming pool. Nudity, while not obligatory, is the norm. The slightly cheaper **Sauna Fenomeen** (ⓐ Eerste Schinkelstraat 14 ⓣ 020 671 6780 ⓦ www.saunafenomeen.nl ⓝ Tram: 1, 2 to Amstelveenseweg) is decorated in bright colours and mosaics and has a vegetarian café. Mondays are women-only.

Accommodation

Amsterdam has hotels of all types and all standards, scattered around the city.

If you're after a lively time and don't mind the noise, look for accommodation around Centraal Station and near to Dam Square. If you like somewhere quieter with more character, search out the Jordaan neighbourhood, or elsewhere around the Canal Ring. Some of the tall canal-side buildings have been converted into atmospheric hotels. Note that they often don't have a lift, so if you have trouble with stairs do check in advance. For an alternative experience you can also stay on the canals, as some boats have been turned into floating B&Bs. The Museum Quarter is fine if you will only be visiting a short time and plan to spend it all visiting the main museums, but the area is somewhat lacking in character. Bear in mind that the city's attractions are easily reached on foot pretty much no matter where you stay.

A continental breakfast is usually included in the price of a room.

HOTELS

Acacia £ Right by a canal in the Jordaan district. No lift. The friendly owners also rent out rooms in two nearby canal boats. ⓐ Lindengracht 251 ⓣ 020 622 1460 ⓦ www.hotelacacia.nl ⓝ Bus: 18 to Willemstraat

PRICE CATEGORIES
Ratings are based on the average cost of a standard room for two people for one night.
£ up to €99   ££ €100–€199   £££ over €200

BOOK EARLY

Amsterdam is a small, old city but a popular one and there isn't really enough accommodation to deal with the huge numbers of visitors flocking to it. Book well ahead, especially at weekends and in summer, and don't expect to find anything really cheap. Even in winter, when room rates drop and you can sometimes find special deals, you should still plan ahead. Turning up in Amsterdam without booking a room in advance is definitely not recommended.

Amstel Botel £ This floating hotel in the dock by Centraal Station couldn't be more central, though it can be a bit noisy. A bargain for 3-star comfort. ⓐ Oosterdokskade 2–4 ⓣ 020 626 4247 ⓦ www.amstelbotel.nl Ⓝ Five-min. walk from Centraal Station

Bicycle Hotel Amsterdam £ Friendly, affordable hotel in a great neighbourhood offering bike rental. ⓐ Van Ostadestraat 123 ⓣ 020 679 3452 ⓦ www.bicyclehotel.com Ⓝ Tram: 4, 25 to Ceintuurbaan/Sarphatipark

Winston £ Arty and edgy but affordable, the Winston is located on Amsterdam's oldest street. Each hotel room has been designed differently by artists around the world – everything from Gothic chambers to Polaroid wallpaper – which makes for a unique experience. A word of warning: the hotel is loud as there's a bar directly downstairs and it lies on the border of the red light district. ⓐ Warmoesstraat 123 ⓣ 020 623 1380 ⓦ www.winston.nl Ⓝ Short walk from Centraal Station

Bridge Hotel £–££ Right on the Amstel River where it crosses the Canal Ring, this hotel is slightly out of the centre in a quiet area. Good-sized comfortable rooms. ➊ Amstel 107–111 ➊ 020 623 7068 Ⓦ www.thebridgehotel.nl Ⓝ Tram: 9; Metro: 50, 51, 53 to Waterlooplein

Canal House ££ Three 17th-century canal houses, stylishly converted without losing their historic feel. ➊ Keizersgracht 148 ➊ 020 622 5182 Ⓦ www.canalhouse.nl Ⓝ Tram: 1, 2, 5, 6, 13, 17 to Dam Square

Keizershof ££ A converted 1672 canal house with beamed rooms, though the authentic historical feel means that not all rooms are en suite. Great character and breakfast. ➊ Keizersgracht 618 ➊ 020 622 2855 Ⓦ www.hotelkeizershof.nl Ⓝ Tram: 16, 24, 25 to Keizersgracht

Lloyd Hotel & Cultural Embassy ££ Located in the fashionable Docklands area just east of Centraal Station, Lloyd offers open spaces, harbour views and unconventional décor. Choose from 3- to 5-star, depending on your pocket or mood. ➊ Oostelijke Handelskade 34 ➊ 020 561 3636 Ⓦ www.lloydhotel.com Ⓝ Tram: 26 to Rietlandpark

Seven Bridges ££ Near the Amstel River, with views of seven bridges, this old canal house has antique décor and makes for an affordable yet stylish stay. ➊ Reguliersgracht 31 ➊ 020 623 1329 Ⓦ www.sevenbridgeshotel.nl Ⓝ Tram: 16, 24, 25 to Keizersgracht

Singel Hotel ££ Friendly hotel overlooking the Singel Canal in a quiet location near Centraal Station. ➊ Singel 13–17 ➊ 020 626 3108 Ⓦ www.singelhotel.nl Ⓝ Short walk from Centraal Station

▶ *An attractive hotel in the city centre*

The Dylan £££ This celebrity hang-out, until recently known as Blakes, is based around a 17th-century former theatre. It is set back from the canal front and decorated in a restrained modern style. ⓐ Keizersgracht 384 ⓣ 020 530 2010 ⓦ www.dylanamsterdam.com ⓝ Tram: 1, 2, 5, 6, 10, 17 to Leidseplein or ten-min. walk from Centraal Station

Pulitzer £££ Perhaps the best treat in Amsterdam for a splurge romantic weekend, the Pulitzer comprises a maze of old canal houses that are now the ultimate in modern comfort. Highly recommended. ⓐ Prinsengracht 315–331 ⓣ 020 523 5235 ⓦ www.pulitzer.nl ⓝ Tram: 13,17, 20; Bus: 21 to Westermarkt

APARTMENTS

Amsterdam House £ This company has several canal-side apartments you can rent by the week plus ten houseboats. Live right among the houseboat-dwellers of Amsterdam for less than it costs to stay in a hotel. ⓐ 's-Gravelandseveer 7 ⓣ 020 626 2577 ⓦ www.amsterdamhouse.com ⓝ Tram: 4, 9, 16, 24, 25 to Munt Tower

Maes B&B £–££ Named after famous Dutch painter Nicholaas Maes, this is one of the city's first B&Bs and is known for its pleasant ambience. Very comfortable, with numerous staircases leading to attractive rooms with big bathrooms. Apartments also available. ⓐ Herenstraat 26 ⓣ 020 427 5165 ⓦ www.bedandbreakfastamsterdam.com ⓝ Short walk from Centraal Station

HOSTELS & CAMPSITES

Camping Het Amsterdamse Bos £ This campsite is fairly far from the city centre but has cabins to rent – Amsterdam can be wet.

ⓐ Kliene Noorddijk 1, Amstelveen ☎ 020 641 6868
ⓦ www.campingamsterdamsebos.nl Ⓝ Bus: 172 to Amstelveen
station, then bus: 171

NJHC City Hostel Vondelpark £ As its name suggests, this hostel is right by the Vondelpark and is handy for both the Museum Quarter and the city centre. ⓐ Zandpad 5 ☎ 020 589 8996 Ⓝ Tram: 1, 2, 5, 6, 10, 17 to Leidseplein

Vliegenbos campsite £ One of the closest campsites to the city centre. ⓐ Meeuwenlaan 138 ☎ 020 636 8855 ⏱ Apr–end Sept Ⓝ Bus: 32, 33, 361. Stop is 200 metres (219 yards) from campsite

🔺 *Amsterdam's beautiful Pulitzer Hotel*

THE BEST OF AMSTERDAM

You'll enjoy Amsterdam no matter how short or long a visit you have. Whether you're after culture, nightlife or the relaxed atmosphere, if time is tight think what your priorities are and don't try to squeeze in too much.

TOP 10 ATTRACTIONS

- **Amsterdams Historisch Museum (Historical Museum)** Lively exploration of the fascinating history of this unique city (see page 66)

- **Anne Frank Huis (Anne Frank House)** This museum and house is an essential (and moving) stop for a first-time visitor to the city (see page 106)

- **Begijnhof** An amazing historical old square – home to the city's oldest house – that survives in the heart of the city (see page 60)

- **Dam Square** This huge square at the heart of Amsterdam is not especially picturesque, but its historical interest cannot be questioned (see page 62)

🔻 *Traditional wooden shoes from Amsterdam*

- **Jordaan district** Once an overcrowded working-class slum, this is now one of the prettiest quarters of the city, relaxing but fun and great for photography (see page 110)

- **Museum Amstelkring** A fascinating historical museum in the heart of the red light district with a once-secret Catholic church at the top (see page 70)

- **De Oude Kerk (The Old Church)** The oldest building in Amsterdam, with stained glass windows from the 1550s, and the finest of the city's several old churches (see page 68)

- **Het Rembrandthuis Museum (The Rembrandt House Museum)** The home and studio of the city's artistic genius. Both ordinary and extraordinary at the same time (see page 70)

- **Rijksmuseum** The grandest of Amsterdam's two most popular art museums, with an unrivalled collection that includes portraits by Dutch masters Rembrandt and Vermeer (see page 96)

- **Van Gogh Museum** People travel from around the world to see this, the finest collection of Van Gogh's work all housed in one place and much else besides (see page 98)

Suggested itineraries

HALF-DAY: AMSTERDAM IN A HURRY

If you only have a few hours, forget the big museums; you'll never do them justice. Instead, walk through the red light district (see page 67) and visit De Oude Kerk (see page 68) (Amsterdam's oldest monument) and Zuider Kerk (a 17th-century church near Waterlooplein). Continue on to the Het Rembrandthuis (see page 70), which you can visit quickly. Then make your way to the Herengracht canal and look for a canal-side café or restaurant.

1 DAY: TIME TO SEE A LITTLE MORE

Start early and beat the crowds at the Rijksmuseum (see page 96) or Van Gogh Museum (see page 98). Then visit the Het Rembrandthuis Museum and red light district, take in Dam Square (see page 62) and head west across four canals to reach the Jordaan district (see page 110). You'll find plenty of shopping opportunities, along with bars and cafés, plus a terrific choice of eating places for an atmospheric evening meal.

2–3 DAYS: TIME TO SEE MUCH MORE

You can take in both of the major museums and more of the Top 10 Attractions. Take time to relax by visiting the Vondelpark (see page 95) or the Plantage (see page 78), with its museums, planetarium and zoo.

LONGER: ENJOYING AMSTERDAM TO THE FULL

You will have time to make use of the good train network and take a train to Rotterdam (see page 130) or The Hague (see page 120) to see another side of Dutch life. You can see more of the 'real' Amsterdam too, outside of the centre, including the fascinating multicultural

SUGGESTED ITINERARIES

district of De Pijp. Start each day with one of the major sights: Rijksmuseum, Van Gogh Museum, Anne Frank House (see page 106). Get there 15 minutes before opening time to avoid the queues.

🔺 *Busy Dam Square is at the heart of the city*

Something for nothing

If you're looking to enjoy Amsterdam without spending too much money, you'll find plenty to do. Some of the top sights in the city are free, such as the Begijnhof (see page 60), the Bloemenmarkt (Flower Market, see page 87) and the hidden treat, the **Hollandsche Manege**, or Dutch Riding School (ⓐ Vondelstraat 140 ⓣ 020 618 0942 ⓦ www.dehollandschemanege.nl ⓝ Tram: 1 to Overtoom).

If you're a party-lover, the best way to enjoy the city inexpensively is to visit during one of its many festivals (see pages 8–11). There are free concerts during the music festivals, such as the Amsterdam Roots Festival (third Sunday in June) and free open-air theatre in the Vondelpark from June to August.

If you're a bargain-hunting museum lover, you should come during the second weekend in April for National Museum Weekend. Entry to the city's museums over the weekend is free, although you'll have to struggle through the crowds.

At other times it's a good idea to buy the Amsterdam city pass, which includes entry to the main museums, public transport and a boat trip.

The canal-side paths make for beautiful strolls and there is always a cheap and cheerful café or bar in which to take a break. Street markets are an endless source of free fun and good photographs. You can put together a picnic at the food markets and take it to one of the city's many parks to stroll, relax and eat. Head to a street stall for some cheap, filling snacks, including the Dutch favourite: herring.

Rollerbladers can join the free Friday Night Skate (see page 33), which starts at the Vondelpark at about 20.00 for a two-hour tour of the city.

Finally there is always the red light district. It's a source of endless fascination for visitors ... and it costs nothing to look.

⬤ *Stop for the obligatory photo on the Magere Brug*

When it rains

It rains a fair bit in Amsterdam. Wet weather is not a problem, though, because the city is used to it. You can still take a trip in a canal boat, for instance, just under cover. You can still enjoy a visit to the Hortus Botanicus (Botanical Gardens) (see page 80) as it has some great indoor greenhouses.

In fact, rain is a good opportunity to linger in the main museums and really admire Rembrandt, Vermeer and Van Gogh's work. When the sun is shining outside, you might be tempted to whizz by the paintings but you'd miss a lot. You can also take the time to visit Amsterdam's countless smaller museums and churches, which are more quietly spectacular. The modern science museum NEMO (see page 65), will keep you busy for hours.

Wet weather is part of the Dutch lifestyle and looked on as an opportunity to relax. You can join in with the locals by spending longer in the bars and cafés, chatting and taking it easy. The people are friendly and open, so striking up conversations is never difficult. Make the effort and you'll get an insight into the city that most visitors miss because they're too busy rushing around all the sights. The best area to do this is the Jordaan (see page 110), a quiet residential district near the heart of the city. Although popular with visitors, you'll also meet plenty of locals in its wide choice of bars, cafés and restaurants.

Alternatively, make it a shopping day and head to one of several department stores and covered shopping centres. One of the best is at the airport, a 15-minute train ride from Centraal Station to Schiphol.

If the rain looks steady for the day, check to see if the weather's better in Rotterdam or The Hague and jump on a train heading south.

▶ *Stay out of the rain in a covered canal boat*

On arrival

TIME DIFFERENCE

Amsterdam is on Central European Time (CET), one hour ahead of London. Daylight saving applies. Clocks go forward one hour at the end of March and fall back one hour at the end of October.

ARRIVING

By air

Schiphol Airport is 18 km (11 miles) southwest of the city centre and has only one terminal. It has all the usual amenities, including ATMs, duty-free shopping, car hire, ample seating areas, restaurants, as well as a public shopping plaza connected to a bustling train station. It also has a small art museum, an outpost of the Rijksmuseum, just after passport control.

If you haven't booked a hotel, try Booking.com's reservation desk, or the tourist information office located in arrivals lounge 2.

● *Schiphol Airport is a major international hub*

The airport is linked to the city centre by regular trains, which take about 15 minutes to reach Centraal Station. There are usually seven trains every hour during the day and about one an hour during the night. Buy your ticket, around €2 each way, from a counter near the station entrance before boarding the train.

The only bus transfer is the Connexxion bus, which takes much longer than the train and only stops at certain city centre hotels. It will stop at other hotels on request for a charge. You can buy tickets from the tourist information office.

Taxis also take longer than trains to reach the city centre and cost several times more. Unless you have a huge amount of luggage it is cheaper to get a train to Centraal Station, then take a taxi from there to your accommodation. ⓐ Evert van de Beekstraat 202 ⓣ 020 601 9111 ⓦ www.schiphol.nl

By rail

Amsterdam's main station **Amsterdam Centraal** (or Central Station) is located – as the name implies – in the centre of the city's loop of canals, with its back to the Ij waterfront. Most trains to and from Amsterdam, both national and international, start here.

All trains within the Netherlands are operated by the **Nederlandse Spoorwegen** or NS, which means Dutch Railways (ⓦ www.ns.nl). To avoid long queues, use the ticket machines around the station, which offer an English-language option but often don't accept foreign credit or debit cards. There are also regular ticket booths. While tickets to Brussels and Germany can be bought from machines, most will have to be booked from the international ticket booth, located on platform 2b. Don't forget to buy a ticket, regardless of your destination. Tickets cannot be bought on board and you'll face an immediate €35 fine if caught.

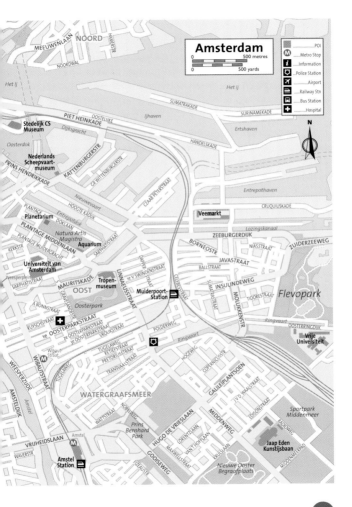

Amsterdam

0		500 metres
0		500 yards

- ▦ ....POI
- Ⓜ ....Metro Stop
- 🛈 ....Information
- ▣ ....Police Station
- ✈ ....Airport
- ▤ ....Railway Stn
- ▤ ....Bus Station
- ✚ ....Hospital

MEEUWENLAAN

NOORD

HAMERSTR

NOORDWAL

Het IJ

Het IJ

SUMATRAKADE

SURINAMEKADE

PIET HEINKADE

OOSTELIJKE

IJhaven

Ertshaven

Stedelijk CS Museum

Dijksgracht

Oosterdok

HANDELSKADE

N

Nederlands Scheepvaart-museum

KATTENBURGERSTR

GH WITTENBURGERSTR

CZAAR PETERSTRAAT

Entrepothaven

PRINS HENDRIKKADE

Nieuwevaart

HOOGTE KADIJK

CRUQUIUSKADE

PLANTAGE

Entrepotdok

DOKLAAN

Planetarium

Veemarkt

Natura Artis Magistra

PLANTAGE MIDDENLAAN

ZEEBURGERDIJK

PLANTAGE MUIDERGRACHT

KERKSTR

Aquarium

SARPHATISTRAAT

BORNEOSTR

NIASSTRAAT

ZUIDERZEEWEG

Lozingskanaal

Universiteit van Amsterdam

JAVASTRAAT

Weesperplein

JAFFER STRAAT

1e V. SWINDENSTRAAT

BALLSTRAAT

INSULINDEWEG

SARPHATISTRAAT

MAURITSKADE

GRAVESANDESTR

Tropen-museum

SUMATRASTRAAT

Flevopark

OOST

LINNAEUSSTRAAT

CELEBESSTR

MOLUKKENSTR

TIDORESTRAAT

Muiderpoort-Station

Oosterpark

A BONNSTRAAT

RUYSCHSTRAAT

POLDERWEG

OOSTERRINGDIJK

1e OOSTERPARKSTRAAT

Ringvaart

Vrije Universiteit

2e OOSTERPARKSTRAAT

VROLIKSTRAAT

HOGEWEG

2e OOSTERPARKSTRAAT

Wibaut straat

TUGELAWEG

RETIEFSTRAAT

Ringvaart

WEESPERZIJDE

Amstel

TUGELAWEG

PRETORIUSSTRAAT

KOPENHAGEN STR

WIBAUTSTRAAT

TRANSVAALSTRAAT

WATERGRAAFSMEER

GALILEÏPLANTSOEN

AMSTELDIJK

NOBELWEG

WATTSTRAAT

J.v.d. WAALSLAAN

Sportpark Middenmeer

Prins Bernhard Park

HUGO DE VRIESLAAN

MIDDENWEG

LORENTZLAAN

RADIOWEG

VAN 'T HOFFLAAN

EDISONSTRAAT

VRIJHEIDSLAAN

Amstel

Jaap Eden Kunstijsbaan

MAXWELLSTRAAT

KRUISLAAN

MIDDENMEERPAD

WAVERSTR

GOOISEWEG

TELEAUSTR

Amstel Station

Nieuwe Ooster Begraafplaats

Centraal Station has been undergoing construction works for years, as the city builds a new metro extension. Allow plenty of time and expect to see signs and detours directing you elsewhere. The station has the usual ATMs, shops, restaurants and fast-food places and a bureau de change. In the open square in front of the station you'll find buses, trams, taxis and a tourist information office. There are metro links to Nieuwmarkt and Waterlooplein.

Lost property (ⓐ Stationsplein 15 ⓣ 020 557 85 44) keeps items for three days before shipping them to Utrecht. You'll need ID to reclaim anything.

By road

Amsterdam's most central terminus for its bus and tram network is directly outside Centraal Station. The city's public transport service, **GVB** (ⓣ 020 460 6060), has an office here where you can get maps and information, and buy tickets for travel in the city centre and suburbs.

Regional buses are operated by **Connexxion** (ⓣ 0900 266 6399 ⓦ www.connexxion.nl) and **Arriva** (ⓣ 0900 202 2022 ⓦ www.arriva.nl). The regional bus station is on Marnixstraat, which is fairly central.

International Eurolines coaches arrive at Amstel station, which is linked to the city centre by train as well as by metro lines 51, 53 and 54 and by tram line 12.

Driving in Amsterdam is not recommended: crowded, narrow streets, looping concentric canals and one-way systems traversing this already compact city guarantee regular traffic. If you do drive, expect to have trouble finding parking in the centre. Some public car parks can be found at:

P1 Parking Amsterdam Centre ⓐ Prins Hendrikkade 20A
P1 Parking Waterlooplein ⓐ Valkenburgerstraat 238
Q Park Byzantium ⓐ Tesselschadestraat 1G
Q Park Museumplein ⓐ Van Baerlestraat 33B

FINDING YOUR FEET

Amsterdam is a traveller-friendly city. Almost everyone speaks English, in addition to several other languages, and people are willing to help with directions and information if you need it.

Amsterdam is generally a pleasant and safe place to wander round and fairly easy to navigate with the aid of a good map. Like any big city there is crime. Take special care around Centraal Station, which attracts pickpockets and petty thieves. Likewise, keep an eye on your wallet or handbag in the red light district.

In particular, beware the cyclists. They do pedal fast and because many junctions along the canals are four-way it is important to look in every direction. Keep an eye out for the trams, too. It's easy to forget they are there.

ORIENTATION

The city centre can seem confusing at first, as one *gracht*, or canal, looks much like another. The way that several canals circle the city centre in a horseshoe shape also means you might get easily confused

---

IF YOU GET LOST, TRY ...

Do you speak English?
Spreekt u Engels?
Spraykt-oo Eng-els?

Is this the way to...?
Is dit de weg naar...?
Is dit de vekh naar...?

Could you point it out on the map?
Kunt u het op de kaart aanwijzen?
Kunt oo het op de kaart aan-wayezen?

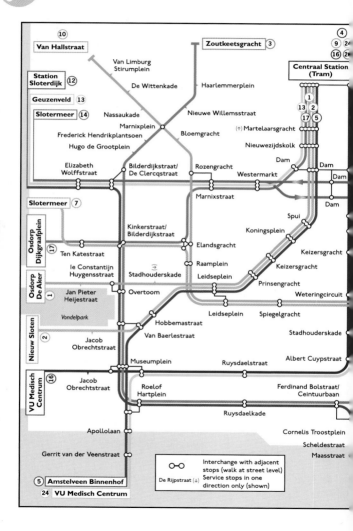

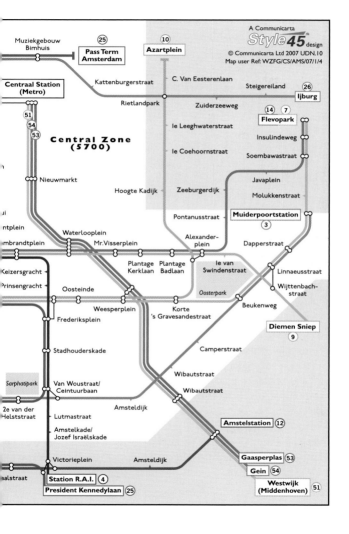

MONEY-SAVING TRAVEL

The best way to save money on public transport is to buy a *nationale strippenkaart* from a tourist office, metro or rail station, or a shop showing the appropriate sign. This gives you 15 or 45 units to spend on any public transport and cuts the cost considerably if you take a few journeys. A central journey usually costs two units. The city's public transport service GVB also offers one-, two- or three-day passes that allow unlimited travel on all trams, buses, metros and night buses. Don't rush into buying, though, until you know where you are staying and how close you are to the attractions you want to see. If the weather's fine, then Amsterdam is an easy and pleasant city to walk around.

about which direction you're facing. That said, many of the sights can be found on or near a canal and walking along one until you reach your destination is a lovely way of getting to know the city.

The four main canals radiate out from the centre in the following order: Singelgracht, Herengracht, Keizersgracht and Prinsengracht. There are hundreds of bridges and smaller canals connecting the larger ones – the good news is that it's great fun getting lost.

Centraal Station is located in the middle of the city's U-shaped canals at the mouth of the Ij waterfront. If you follow the street south you'll find Dam Square – a major meeting point – and further on you'll reach the touristy Leidseplein. This square is slightly above Vondelpark, the biggest park in the city.

The red light district is a five-minute walk from the station, in the area just north of Dam Square, while the Jordaan district lies to the

west. Beyond the canal ring encircling the city is the Museumplein,
or Museum Quarter.

Free maps are hard to come by, but it's worth getting a detailed
one as many of the best finds are on smaller streets running off
the main ones. Several of the tobacconists near Leidseplein sell
city maps.

GETTING AROUND

You can cross Amsterdam on foot in an hour and walking is by far
the most pleasant way of getting around.

In terms of regular public transport, the tram is the easiest and
the most popular option. The tram network covers the city centre,
with 15 lines running regularly until 00.15. When travelling on most
trams you must buy your tickets in advance and validate them on the
tram, or buy a travel pass. Some newer trams have been introduced
with conductors on board; on these you must enter through the
rear doors and show the conductor your tickets, or buy one on board.

There's a metro within the city centre, but its four lines are
mainly used to serve the suburbs. One line travels between Centraal
Station, Nieuwmarkt and Waterlooplein, the only two city centre
stops likely to interest visitors. A new line should be open by 2011.

Buses are more useful for venturing further afield, although
there are some city centre bus routes. There are night buses in the
centre running from midnight to 07.00, along routes that connect
to Centraal Station, Rembrandtplein and Leidseplein.

It is a good idea to pick up a free *English-language Tourist Guide
to Public Transport* from the tourist office outside Centraal Station
when you first arrive. It explains everything you need to know.

Taxis are best picked up at taxi ranks on major road junctions
and outside the main hotels. You can flag one down in the street

MUSEUM BOAT

It makes a pleasant change to travel across the city on the canals using the Amsterdam Museum Boat. The boat operates all day and you can hop on or off the boat as much as you like. There are stops at attractions such as the Stopera, Rijksmuseum, Anne Frank House, Scheepvaartmuseum (Maritime Museum) as well as Centraal Station. Tickets also include up to 50 per cent reduction on museum entrance fees.

You can find out more details and buy tickets from any tourist information office.

if you see an empty one. Common practice for tipping is to round up the fare to the nearest convenient amount.

CAR HIRE

There is no need to hire a car if you plan to stay in the city. If you want a car to explore further afield, it's easiest to rent one at Schiphol Airport. Agencies based there include Avis, Budget, Hertz, National Car Rental and Sixt. In the centre, try:

Alamo ⓐ Overtoom 184 ⓣ 020 616 2466 ⓦ www.alamo.com
Avis ⓐ Nassaukade 380 ⓣ 0900 235 2847 ⓦ www.avis.nl
Hertz ⓐ Overtoom 333 ⓣ 020 612 2441 ⓦ www.hertz.com
Tiger ⓦ www.tigercarrental.com

● *Amsterdam may be easier to get around by foot or bicycle*

Central Amsterdam

Central Amsterdam, sometimes called the old town or the medieval quarter, is the heart of the city. Here you'll find the main railway station, the main square, several museums, old churches and the infamous red light district. Several of the major sights in the city are located in the area, in particular the unmissable Rembrandthuis (Rembrandt's House).

As well as the inevitable modern buildings, hotels, restaurants and shops you'll come across lovely traditional churches and narrow gabled buildings in the side streets. Amsterdam is an old but vibrant city, where traditional and modern styles thrive together. De Oude Kerk (The Old Church), for example, the oldest building in Amsterdam, sits right in the heart of the brash, neon-lit red light district.

SIGHTS & ATTRACTIONS

Amsterdam Centraal (Central Station)

As well as being a major transport hub, Centraal Station is an attraction in its own right as a fine example of late 19th-century architecture. It was designed by Petrus Josephus Hubertus Cuypers, the same architect who built the Rijksmuseum. Built on three specially created artificial islands and resting on 30,000 pylons, the station was originally a source of controversy as it separated the city from the river for the first time. But like many controversial buildings, time has allowed it to win over the hearts of the local people. ⓐ Stationsplein ⓘ 020 557 8400 Ⓜ Metro to Centraal Station; Tram: 1, 2, 4, 5, 6, 9, 13, 16, 17, 24, 25

Begijnhof

This square is not only an amazing, quiet oasis right in the middle of the bustle of Amsterdam, but contains the oldest house in the

Central Amsterdam

0 ━━━━━ 250 metres
0 ━━━━━ 250 yards

N

Het IJ

Panama

KATTENBURGERSTR

HENKADE

PIET HENKADE

DIJKSGRACHT

Dijks Gracht

DIJKSGRACHT

KATTENBURGERGRACHT

Nieuwevaart

HOOGTE KADIJK

Aquarium

Nederlands
Scheepvaart-
museum

Stedelijk CS
Museum

newMetropolis
Museum

KATTENBURGER-
PLEIN

WITTENBURGERGRACHT

Entrepotdok

Natura Artis
Magistra

PRINS HENDRIKKADE

PLANTAGE DOKLAN

Planetarium

DE RUITERKADE

OOSTERDOKSKADE

Oosterdok

OOSTERDOKSKADE

PLANTAGE MIDDENLAAN

Central
Museum

Centraal
Station

PRINS HENDRIKKADE

BINNENKANT

Wert-
heim
park

NIEUWE HEERENGRACHT

PLANTAGE MUIDERGRACHT

KAZERNESTR

❶

Café du Lac

Bitterzoet

Belgique

PRINS HENDRIKKADE

ROSSE BUURT
(RED LIGHT DISTRICT)

ZEEDIJK

Museum
Amstelkring

Oude
Kerk

❸

VOORBURGWAL

NIEUWENDIJK

WARMOESSTRAAT

DAMRAK

Ouderzijds Voorburgwal

ACHTERBURGWAL

KONINGSTRAAT

Nieuwmarkt

❽

Maximiliaan

ST ANTONIESBREESTRAAT

Zuiderkerk

Joods Historisch
Museum

WEESPERSTRAAT

Het Rembrandthuis
Museum

Stadhuis

Amstelhof

Opera

Amstel

NIEUWMARKT

Kloveniersburgwal

JODENBREESTRAAT

DANSTRAAT

RUSLAND

Tassenmuseum
Hendrikje

Allard Pierson
Museum

❶

❾

❷

❺

❹

❶❶

Amsterdams
Historisch
Museum

Begijnhof

Universiteit
van Amsterdam

ROKIN

KALVERSTRAAT

NES

SPUI

SPUISTRAAT

Singel

Katten Kabinet

Bloemenmarkt

MUNTPLEIN

VIJZELSTRAAT

VIJZELSTRAAT

HERENGRACHT

❶❷

SINGEL

SINGEL

Herengracht

Herengracht

Herengracht

Keizersgracht

Keizersgracht

Keizersgracht

Prinsengracht

Prinsengracht

Prinsengracht

Anne Frank Huis

PC Hooftstraat

RAADHUISSTRAAT

NIEUWEZIJDS VOORBURGWAL

NIEUWEZIJDS VOORBURGWAL

SPUISTRAAT

DAM SQUARE

❶❺

❶❸

❼

❻

❶❶

❶❻

Bloemgracht

ROZENGRACHT

ELANDSGRACHT

LAURIERGRACHT

PRINSENGRACHT

KEIZERSGRACHT

HERENGRACHT

ROKIN

REGULIERSGRACHT

KERKSTRAAT

❻

Key	
Ⓜ	Metro Stop
ⓘ	Information
Ⓟ	Police Station
✈	Airport
🚂	Railway Stn
⬛	Bus Station
✚	Hospital

city. To find it, take the narrow, gated alleyway on the north side of Spui, at no. 14. Alternatively, until 17.00 you can reach it from the Amsterdams Historisch Museum (see feature box on page 66).

The square has been here since 1346, when it was used as part of a convent for the Beguines order. This was a more liberal order than most, as the nuns did not have to take the usual vows of poverty, chastity and obedience and were allowed to own property while also doing their good works for the poor and the sick. The original buildings have gone, but the garden and courtyard are still surrounded by some of Amsterdam's finest and oldest buildings.

No. 34 is Het Houten Huis (Wooden House), which dates back to about 1470 or earlier and is one of the most photographed sights in the city. No. 30 conceals a secret chapel, built in 1671, which you can visit.

There are no nuns here these days. The last member of the order to live here died in 1971; the grand houses are now rented out to female students and elderly women. ⓐ Gedempte Begijnensloot, off Spui ⓦ www.begijnhofamsterdam.nl ⓛ 13.00–18.30 Mon, 09.00–18.30 Tues–Fri, 09.00–18.00 Sat & Sun ⓝ Tram: 1, 2, 4, 5, 9, 14, 16, 24, 25 to Spui

Dam Square

Dam Square, known simply as the Dam, is the location of the original 13th-century dam across the Amstel river that gives the city its name. The square, once a large fish market, has gradually became the hub of city life. While no-one would pretend it is one of the most picturesque squares in the world it is a great spot for people-watching. Take care crossing the large square as tourists, locals, bikes and vehicles of all kinds come at you from several directions.

❱ *Centraal Station is a fine building in its own right*

Look out for the massive **Koninklijk Paleis (Royal Palace)** dominating the west end of the square. It looks more like a civic building than a royal residence, which it is in part, but the Dutch monarchy are as laid-back as the rest of the population. The Queen remains immensely popular for her down-to-earth approach to life. The Palace is occasionally open for tours, but the days and times are erratic.

Near the Palace stands the **Nieuwe Kerk (New Church)**. The name is misleading. The church dates from the 16th century and therefore is only new in relation to the Oude Kerk (Old Church).

Also in Dam Square, at the far end from the church and Palace, is the **Nationaal Monument**, commemorating the citizens of Amsterdam

● *The striking newMetropolis Museum (NEMO)*

who suffered during the Nazi occupation of World War II. Tram: 1, 2, 4, 5, 6, 9, 13, 14, 16, 17, 24, 25

newMetropolis Museum (NEMO)

There's no mistaking the newMetropolis Museum, or NEMO. It looks uncannily like a giant ship, or even a green spaceship, as you approach it from the bridge across the Oosterdok southeast of Centraal Station. The controversial structure was designed by Renzo Piano and is worth a visit even if only to see the view over Amsterdam from its roof.

NEMO is a science and technology centre with three floors of interactive exhibits. You can learn anything from how light and sound waves work, to how cheese is made, to how to perform a surgical operation. This place is fun for kids of all ages. ⓐ Oosterdok 2 ⓣ 020 531 3233

📞 020 531 3535 🌐 www.e-nemo.nl ✉ info@e-nemo.nl 🕐 10.00–17.00
Tues–Sun, Sept–May; 10.00–17.00 Mon–Sun, June–Aug & school
holidays Ⓜ Metro to Centraal Station; Bus: 22, 32. Admission charge

HISTORY LESSON

Amsterdam's fascinating history of ships and the sea, of spices,
diamonds and – more recently – sex, drugs and rock and roll,
is explored in Amsterdam's excellent and newly renovated
Amsterdams Historisch Museum (Historical Museum). It's
a great place to visit at the start of a trip.

The building itself is part of history. A convent in the 16th
century, it later became an orphanage and the museum is divided
into two by the trench that once separated boys from girls.

Follow the galleries and you see Amsterdam develop from
a tiny fishing village at the start of the 13th century through
to its heyday in the 17th century. It was the damming of the
Amstel River, originally done to reduce flooding, which led to
this development; ships were forced to unload their cargoes
here, creating jobs and making the town a trading centre.

The city's unique artistic and cultural movements arose
from the expansion of its trade and industry and the recent
influx of foreign workers. The museum follows the city's
history right through to the present day and gives you a
good idea of what makes Amsterdam tick. 📍 Kalverstraat 92,
Nieuwezijds Voorburgwal 357 📞 020 523 1822 📠 020 620 7789
🌐 www.ahm.nl ✉ info@ahm.amsterdam.nl 🕐 10.00–17.00
Mon–Fri, 11.00–17.00 Sat, Sun & holidays 🚊 Tram: 1, 2, 5 to Spui;
Tram: 4, 9, 14, 16, 24, 25 to Rokin. Admission charge

Rosse Buurt/De Wallen (Red Light District)

The red light district is usually the one area of a city most visitors avoid. In Amsterdam it's the opposite; the place is filled not only with prostitutes and live sex shows but with tourists who come simply to stand and stare. The girls sit openly in the windows of little apartments, dressed or, more accurately, undressed, in a range of outrageous and skimpy outfits. It is not a place to go if you are easily shocked.

The area itself would be quite a picturesque part of Amsterdam, with its narrow canal-side streets, but it is not a good idea to get your camera out. The girls, and their protectors in the streets outside, don't take kindly to having their picture taken. Remember to watch out for pickpockets and be prepared to see some unpleasant sights on account of a persistent drug problem. By and large, though, the police and city authorities do a good job of keeping the area safe for visitors.

ⓐ Roughly south of Zeedijk, north of Damstraat and east of Damrak
Ⓜ Metro to Nieuwmarkt; Tram: 4, 9, 14, 16, 20, 24, 25

Tassenmuseum Hendrikje (Museum of Bags and Purses)

An unusual museum showcasing women's handbags and purses throughout Western history, this is a bit like walking into a movie star's wardrobe. The collection encompasses around 3,500 bags, pouches, suitcases and the like, from the medieval ages to contemporary designs. It offers an insight into the bag's function as well as the variety of shapes and materials they're made of. Even better, the museum shop offers a large array of bags by contemporary Dutch and foreign designers. It is hard to resist buying one after being taunted by so many fashionable examples. ⓐ Herengracht 573 ⓣ 020 524 6452 ⓦ www.tassenmuseum.nl ⓛ 10.00–17.00 Ⓜ Metro to Waterlooplein. Admission charge

Zuiderkerk

Near the Rembrandt House Museum is the Zuiderkerk, a grand
Gothic construction built in 1611. Its high tower is open in summer
for those who can manage all the steps and has great views. The
tower entrance is outside the church, which is now the Amsterdam
council's information and display centre. ⓐ Zandstraat ❶ 020 689 2565
🕓 Church 12.00–17.00 Mon–Wed & Fri, 12.00–20.00 Thur; Tower by
tour only 12.00–15.30 Mon–Sat, Apr–Sept. Tours every 30 min, 15 people
per tour Ⓜ Metro to Waterlooplein. Admission charge for tower

CULTURE

De Oude Kerk (The Old Church)

If you only see one church in Amsterdam make it this one, the Old
Church in the heart of the red light district. There's been a church on
this spot since the mid-13th century, although the present building
dates back to the mid-14th century. The highlights of the church are
its wonderful stained-glass windows, some of which date back as far
as the 1550s. When the light is bright they are stunningly beautiful, a
complete contrast to the bright lights and neon in the streets around.

The church's interior these days is used for art displays and other
shows and it is a venue for regular music concerts. Look for notices
advertising the concerts and try to go, as it's quite an experience to
sit and enjoy music here. ⓐ Oudekerksplein 23 ❶ 020 625 8284
Ⓦ www.oudekerk.nl 🕓 11.00–17.00 Mon–Sat, 13.00–17.00 Sun
Ⓣ Tram: 4, 9, 16, 20, 24, 25

Katten Kabinet (Cat Cabinet)

The death of his favourite cat sparked the founder of the Cat Cabinet
to open what is probably the world's only museum featuring an art

collection focused solely on cats. Even allergic feline lovers can visit, as the cats here are painted ones, but there's more to see than just fur. The museum is located in a building dating back to 1667, which once housed Amsterdam's mayor and welcomed visitors such as American president John Adams. You can see its original ballroom and music chambers. ⓐ Herengracht 497 ☎ 020 626 5378 ⓦ www.kattenkabinet.nl ⏰ 10.00–14.00 Tues–Fri, 13.00–17.00 Sat & Sun Ⓝ Tram: 1. Admission charge

⬤ *The historic spire of De Oude Kerk*

Museum Amstelkring

One of the most fascinating museums in the city is the Amstelkring, set in a 17th-century merchant's house in the heart of the red light district. Its location makes it all the more surprising that hidden in the upper floors is a complete Catholic church, built at a time when Catholics needed to be careful in Protestant Amsterdam. Shoe-horned into this small space, there is no evidence of a church visible from outside – a condition of its existence. Catholics were allowed to hold services in private buildings provided nothing outside indicated their presence. There were several such churches in Amsterdam, but this is the only one to survive in its original state.

The lower three floors of the museum are given over to displays of what life was like in a merchant's house such as this one, which was built, complete with church, in 1663. There are also displays of religious art and the house itself is intriguing for its warren-like nature. ⓐ Oudezijds Voorburgwal 40 ⓣ 020 624 6604 ⓕ 020 638 1822 ⓦ www.museumamstelkring.nl ⓔ info@museumamstelkring.nl ⓛ 10.00–17.00 Mon–Sat, 13.00–17.00 Sun & holidays ⓝ Metro to Centraal Station; Tram: 4, 9, 16, 20, 24, 25. Admission charge

Het Rembrandthuis Museum (The Rembrandt House Museum)

To see a Rembrandt painting in the Rijksmuseum is one thing, but to visit his actual house and see the studio where he worked is quite an experience. The artist bought the house in 1639 and lived there for just over 20 years at the peak of his fame. He spent so much money furnishing the house, however, that he was eventually declared bankrupt and had to move to a more modest home in the Jordaan, a working-class neighbourhood at the time.

It is fascinating to see the kitchen and, of course, the studio where the artist worked. There's also a room displaying objects that Rembrandt collected and studied: sculptures, stones, feathers and anything that interested him for its shape, texture or colour. There is a collection of the artist's work in a separate annexe, though these are mostly sketches. For his best works you need to visit the Rijksmuseum (see page 96).

The building is a fine, three-storey affair, but it can get crowded as some of the rooms are fairly small. Go early or late in the day if you can. ⓐ Jodenbreestraat 4–6 ⓣ 020 520 0400 ⓕ 020 520 0401 ⓦ www.rembrandthuis.nl ⓔ museum@rembranthuis.nl ⓛ 10.00–17.00 ⓣ Tram: 9, 14; Museumboat. Admission charge

RETAIL THERAPY

The centre of Amsterdam has all the shops typical of any major metropolis, plus a few specialist shops you'd be hard pushed to find anywhere else.

Amsterdam Diamond Centre The biggest diamond shop in the centre of the city, it also sells other jewellery and conventional souvenirs. Take a diamond tour before buying. ⓐ Rokin 1–5 ⓣ 020 624 5787 ⓛ 09.30–18.00 Fri–Wed, 09.30–20.30 Thur

Condomerie This shop, which specialises in condoms, has to be seen to be believed. ⓐ Warmoesstraat 141 ⓣ 020 627 4174 ⓦ www.condomerie.nl ⓛ 11.00–18.00 Mon–Sat ⓝ Tram: 1, 2, 5 to Spui

De Bijenkorf Probably the most famous department store in the Netherlands, you'll realise why it's called 'The Beehive' if you visit. ⓐ Dam 1 ⓣ 020 621 8080 ⓦ www.bijenkorf.nl ⓛ 11.00–19.00 Mon, 09.30–19.00 Tues, Wed, Fri & Sat, 09.30–21.00 Thur, 12.00–18.00 Sun

Dom Brimming with both tasteful and tacky home décor ideas.
ⓐ Spuistraat 281 ☎ 020 428 5544 Ⓦ www.dom-ck.com 🕐 10.00–20.00
Mon–Sat Ⓣ Tram: 1, 2, 5 to Spui

Magic Mushroom Gallery This shop sells drug paraphernalia including
magic mushroom joints. Don't try taking them through customs.
ⓐ Spuistraat 249 ☎ 020 427 5765 Ⓦ www.magicmushroom.com
🕐 11.00–22.00 Sun–Thur, 10.00–22.00 Fri & Sat Ⓣ Tram: 1, 2, 5 to Spui

Magna Plaza Amsterdam's first shopping centre, incorporated into the
city's old post office. ⓐ Nieuwezijds Voorburgwal 182 ☎ 020 626 9199
Ⓦ www.magnaplaza.nl 🕐 11.00–19.00 Mon, 10.00–19.00 Tues, Wed,
Fri & Sat, 10.00–21.00 Thur, 12.00–19.00 Sun Ⓣ Tram: 1, 2, 5, 13, 14, 17;
Bus: 170, 172

TAKING A BREAK

You'll find plenty of choices in the city centre and more fast-food
places here than anywhere else in Amsterdam. Try Rokin, the
major street leading to Dam Square, Leidsestraat, which starts
at Leidseplein, and the bustling Nieuwmarkt square for cafés,
fast-food and ice cream parlours.

Café de Jaren £ ❶ Fine example of a grand café. Overlooking the
Amstel, it manages to be both arty and down to earth at the same
time. ⓐ Nieuwe Doelenstraat 20 ☎ 020 625 5771 🕐 10.00–23.00
Sun–Thur, 10.00–24.00 Fri & Sat Ⓣ Tram: 16 to Muntplein

Café Gollem £ ❷ One of the city's colourful brown cafés with an
especially good collection of beers. ⓐ Raamsteeg 4 ☎ 020 626 6645

🕸 www.cafegollem.nl 🕐 16.00–01.00 Mon–Fri, 14.00–02.00 Sat & Sun
🚊 Tram: 1, 2, 5 to Spui

De Bakkerswinkel £ ❸ Always bustling and crowded, this tea
room at the edge of the red light district is hectic but charming.
🅰 Warmoesstraat 69 📞 020 489 8000 🕸 www.bakkerswinkel.nl
🕐 08.00–16.00 Mon–Fri, 10.00–18.00 Sat, 10.00–17.00 Sun
🚊 Tram: 1, 2, 5 to Spui

Dolores £ ❹ An organic snack bar set up in a converted tram shed,
Dolores serves a variety of organic fare including veggie burgers and
other healthy, reasonably priced snacks. 🅰 Nieuwezijds Voorburgwal,
opposite no. 289 🕐 11.00–22.00 🚊 Tram: 1, 2, 5 to Spui; Tram: 13 to
NZ Voorburgwal

Hoppe £ ❺ This is another of the city's great brown cafés. It dates
back to 1670 and the 17th-century atmosphere remains. While the
main aim is to serve alcohol, you can also get a simple snack here.
🅰 Spuistraat 18–20 📞 020 420 4420 🕐 07.30–01.00 Sun–Thur,
07.30–02.00 Fri & Sat 🚊 Tram: 1, 2, 5 to Spui

Maoz £ ❻ Amsterdam is the place to find falafel and Maoz is the
place to eat it. This spankingly clean chain restaurant is cheap and
the staff are exceedingly cheerful. 🅰 Leidsestraat 85 📞 020 625 0717
🕸 www.maozveg.com 🕐 11.00–01.00 Sun–Thur, 11.00–03.00 Fri & Sat
🚊 Tram: 1, 2, 5, 6, 10, 17 to Leidseplein

Café Luxembourg £–££ ❼ An excellent meeting place, lunch stop
or coffee/beer break, this grand café with a terrace overlooking Spui
Square is one of the city's places to see and be seen in. 🅰 Spuistraat 24

① 020 620 6264 **⏰** 09.00–01.00 Sun–Thur, 09.00–02.00 Fri & Sat
🚊 Tram: 1, 2, 5 to Spui

In de Waag £–££ **❽** This is a great café/restaurant in the Waag,
the medieval city gate dominating Nieuwmarkt square. There is
internet access so you can check your emails too. **📍** Nieuwmarkt 4
① 020 422 7772 **🌐** www.indewaag.nl **⏰** 10.00–24.00 **🚇** Metro: 51, 53,
54 to Nieuwemarkt

AFTER DARK

RESTAURANTS
Kapitein Zeppos £ **❾** An excellent venue serving Flemish and French
cuisine, Zeppos is hidden away down a narrow, cobbled alley. Live
music on Sundays. **📍** Gebed Zonder End 5 **①** 020 624 2057
🌐 www.zeppos.nl **⏰** 10.30–01.00 Mon–Fri, 10.30–02.00 Sat,
16.00–01.00 Sun **🚊** Tram: 9, 16 to Muntplein

Nam Kee £ **❿** One of the city's best-known Chinese restaurants,
located in the red light district but popular with Dutch and
Chinese locals and tourists alike. **📍** Zeedijk 111–113 **①** 020 624 3470
🌐 www.namkee.nl **⏰** 11.30–24.00 **🚇** Metro: 51, 53, 54 to Nieuwmarkt

Pannenkoekhuis £ **⓫** Located up a steep staircase, this tiny restaurant
serving traditional Dutch cuisine is a real time warp. Reservations
recommended. **📍** Grimburgwal 2 **①** 020 626 5603 **⏰** 12.00–19.00
Mon–Fri, 12.00–18.00 Sat, 12.00–17.00 Sun **🚊** Tram: 9 to Muntplein

Sherpa £ **⓬** Run by a Nepali, this colourful, simple restaurant offers
the best Nepalese and Tibetan food in town. Though within a stone's

🔺 *The secluded Kapitein Zeppos restaurant*

throw of the touristy Leidseplein, it's often overlooked, which keeps
prices reasonable. ⓐ Korte Leidsedwarsstraat 58 ⓣ 020 623 9495
ⓦ www.sherpa-restaurant.nl ⓒ 16.00–23.00 ⓝ Tram: 1, 2, 5, 7, 10
to Leidseplein

Kantjil and de Tijger £–££ ⓭ There are countless cheap and cheerful
Indonesian places in Amsterdam, but choose the Antelope and the
Tiger if you want to be guaranteed some of the city's best
ethnic food. It's always full, so you may have to wait for a table.
ⓐ Spuistraat 291–293 ⓣ 020 620 0994 ⓒ 16.30–23.00 ⓝ Tram: 1,
2, 5 to Spui; Tram: 13 to NZ Voorburgwal

Me Naam Naan £–££ ⓮ Thai standards such as Pad Thai and Tom
Yam soup and an array of traditional curries pack in the crowds,
so it's best to reserve or face a long wait. ⓐ Koningsstraat 29
ⓣ 020 423 3344 ⓦ www.menaamnaan.nl ⓒ 17.00–22.30 Tues–Sun
ⓝ Metro: 51, 53, 54 to Nieuwmarkt

Supper Club ££–£££ ⓯ Part restaurant, part club and a totally unique
dining experience, the Supper Club has live or taped music, images
projected on the white walls, changing themes and mattresses to
lounge on while you eat. The set meal is served by attractive young
waiters and waitresses and lasts about four hours. The food is good
rather than brilliant and it's not cheap, but it is a unique night out.
ⓐ Jonge Roelensteeg 21 ⓣ 020 344 6400 ⓦ www.supperclub.nl
ⓒ 20.00–01.00 ⓝ Tram: 1, 2, 4, 5, 13, 14, 16, 17, 24, 25 to Dam Square

d'Vijff Vlieghen £££ ⓰ d'Vijff Vlieghen (The Five Flies) is named after
the five 17th-century canal houses through which its nine dining
rooms sprawl. It serves traditional Dutch food with a modern twist.

Quite formal, but the old-fashioned atmosphere is very romantic too, so save it for an intimate treat. ⓐ Spuistraat 294–302 ⓣ 020 530 4060 ⓦ www.thefiveflies.com ⓛ 17.30–23.00 ⓝ Tram: 1, 2, 5 to Spui; Tram: 13 to NZ Voorburgwal

BARS & CLUBS

Bitterzoet Club? Bar? Theatre? Experience? Bitterzoet is all of those things, so check out what's happening in its intimate performing space. You might get a DJ or a drama, maybe a film or even poetry. ⓐ Spuistraat 2 ⓣ 020 521 3001 ⓦ www.bitterzoet.com ⓛ 20.00–03.00 Sun–Thur, 20.00–04.00 Fri & Sat ⓝ Short walk from Centraal Station

Café Belgique A beer-lover's paradise, with over 50 Belgian brews all available in one place. Serves snacks too. ⓐ Gravenstraat 2 ⓣ 020 625 1974 ⓛ 12.00–01.00 Sun–Thur, 12.00–03.00 Fri & Sat ⓝ Short walk from Centraal Station

Grand Café du Lac More bar than café, despite the name, this place is popular with locals rather than tourists. Look out for the stuffed alligators. ⓐ Haarlemmerstraat 118 ⓣ 020 624 4265 ⓛ 16.00–01.00 Sun–Wed, 16.00–02.00 Thur–Sat ⓝ Short walk from Centraal Station

Panama Amsterdammers like their multimedia venues, bringing the spirit of the 1960s into the 21st century. The Panama, in an old power station in the docks to the east of Centraal Station, is one of the best of these. There's a bar/restaurant as well as a club and a theatre space. Most nights there's live music at 21.00, then DJs with themed music nights from 23.00 until late. Times vary, so check the programme for details. ⓐ Oostelijke Handelskade 4 ⓣ 020 311 8686 ⓦ www.panama.nl ⓝ Tram: 26 to Rietlandpark

Eastern Canal Ring & Plantage

If you head into the eastern side of the city, usually referred to as the Eastern Canal Ring and the city district of Plantage, you'll see a very different side of Amsterdam to that which most people see. Visitors with limited time on their hands naturally focus on the centre and the big museums. If you're lucky enough to have more time, or just don't like going where everyone else goes, head east.

Here you'll find some of the greenery the city centre lacks, like the large Oosterpark and the Hortus Botanicus. There are some smaller museums, too, which are worth a visit, as well as the city zoo, Amsterdam's most photographed bridge and – Amsterdam wouldn't be Amsterdam without it – Heineken.

SIGHTS & ATTRACTIONS

Artis Zoo

The name of Amsterdam's zoo comes from its Latin motto *Natura Artis Magistra* (Nature, the Mistress of the Arts). This grand old zoo dates back to 1838, although in recent years a lot of work has been carried out to modernise the place and to give the animals more space and more natural living conditions.

The zoo covers 14 hectares (34 acres) of land and holds 6,000 animals. It's a good idea, therefore, to get a map and decide what interests you most. The African Savannah is a popular feature, as are the South American Pampas, the renovated aquarium and the wolf enclosure. Check out the feeding times, too, for tamer creatures like penguins and sea lions as well as for the wilder vultures and crocodiles. ⓐ Plantage Kerklaan 38–40 ⓣ 020 523 3400 ⓕ 020 523 3481 ⓦ www.amsterdamzoo.nl ⓔ info@artis.nl

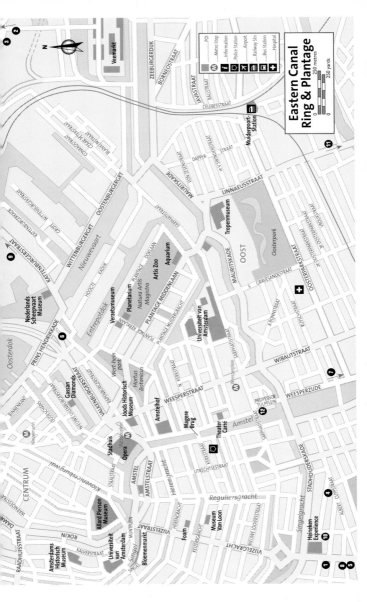

Eastern Canal Ring & Plantage

M	Metro Stop
🄿	POI
ℹ	Information
🏛	Police Station
✈	Airport
🚉	Railway Stn
🚌	Bus Station
✚	Hospital

0 — 250 metres
0 — 250 yards

N

Veemarkt

ZEEBURGERDIJK

BORNEOSTRAAT

CONSTSTRAAT
C&AB PLETSTRAAT
BLANKENSTRAAT

JAVASTRAAT
BALLISTRAAT

CELEBESSTRAAT

Muiderpoort-Station

DAPPER STRAAT

H.J. VAN NASSAUSTRAAT

ZEEBURGERKADE

MAURITSKADE

LINNAEUSSTRAAT

Tropenmuseum

OOST

Oosterpark

S. GRAVESANDESTRAAT

A BONDTSTRAAT

RUISCHSTRAAT

OOSTERPARKSTRAAT

1E OOSTERPARKSTRAAT

2E OOSTERPARKSTRAAT

3E OOSTERPARKSTRAAT

WIBAUTSTRAAT

WEESPERZIJDE

STADHOUDERSKADE

ALBERT CUYPSTRAAT

Singelgracht

Heineken
Experience

VIJZELGRACHT

Museum
Van Loon

Foam

KEIZERSGRACHT

HERENGRACHT

Reguliersgracht

NIEUWE LOOIERSSTRAAT

UTRECHTSESTRAAT

LIJNBAANSGRACHT

PROFESSOR
TULPPLEIN

SARPHATISTRAAT

WEESPERSTRAAT

Amstel

Theater
Carré

Magere
Brug

Amstelhof

Joods Historisch
Museum

Hortus
Botanicus

Wertheim
park

Universiteit van
Amsterdam

PLANTAGE MUIDERGRACHT

PLANTAGE KERKLAAN

PLANTAGE MIDDENLAAN

Natura Artis
Magistra

Artis Zoo

Aquarium

Planetarium

PLANTAGE
DOKLAAN

Verzetsmuseum

Entrepotdok

Nieuwevaart

WITTENBURGERGRACHT

OOSTENBURGERGRACHT

HOOGTE
KADIJK

KATTENBURGERSTRAAT

GROTE WITTENBURGERSTRAAT

PRINS HENDRIKKADE

Nederlands
Scheepvaart
Museum

Oosterdok

Oosterdok

Gassan
Diamonds

VALKENBURGERSTRAAT

NIEUWE UILENBURGERSTRAAT

JODENBREESTRAAT

Stadhuis

Opera

Waterlooplein

Nieuwmarkt

CENTRUM

DAMSTRAAT

WARMOESSTR

RAADHUISSTRAAT

Amsterdams
Historisch
Museum

Universiteit
van
Amsterdam

KALVERSTRAAT

ROKIN

Allard Pierson
Museum

Bloemenmarkt

Muntplein

VIJZELSTRAAT

Singel

Singel

HERENGRACHT

KEIZERSGRACHT

Kloveniersburgwal

AMSTEL

AMSTELSTRAAT

STAATSTRAAT

KERKSTRAAT

🕐 09.00–17.00 (winter); 09.00–18.00 (summer); open until sunset
June–Aug 🚊 Tram: 6, 9, 14, 20. Admission charge

Entrepotdok

Entrepotdok is one of the first and best examples of the way
Amsterdam's docks, fallen into dereliction, have been developed over
the last few decades and turned into fashionable apartments, bars
and restaurants. This was originally a 'free port' in the dock system,
where goods could be moved in and out without incurring taxes
because they were technically not brought ashore in the Netherlands.
It was the biggest warehouse complex in Europe, built by the Dutch
East India Company in the 18th century. Today it's a lovely and
peaceful place to wander round, still full of character and history.
🇦 Entrepotdok 🚌 Bus: 22

Gassan Diamonds

This is one of the best of the many diamond factory tours. At Gassan,
housed in an impressively old building from 1897, you are given a good
free tour of the cutting and polishing rooms and the guides appear
keen to explain the world of diamonds to you. At the end you sit
around a table as the guide shows you different kinds of diamonds.
You can ask as many questions as you like without necessarily buying.
Of course they'd love it if you did and many visitors do. 🇦 Nieuwe
Uilenburgerstraat 173–175 ☎ 020 622 5333 🖶 020 624 6084
🌐 www.gassandiamonds.com ✉ info@gassandiamonds.nl
🕐 09.00–17.00 🚊 Tram: 9, 14, 20

Hortus Botanicus (Botanical Garden)

You don't normally think of botanical gardens as places of great
historical interest, but this one goes right back to 1638 when the

● *The fashionable Entrepotdok area*

HEINEKEN EXPERIENCE

The Heineken Experience is housed on the grounds of the company's former brewery, where Heineken was made from 1864 until 1988, and is one of the city's most popular attractions. It is no longer a working brewery but offers tours in which you can learn how the brewing process works, follow the life of a bottle of Heineken, watch old television advertisements and meet the company's shire horses. It's all done very professionally, with liberal doses of humour, and the admission charge goes to charity. Allow a couple of hours at least, depending on how long you want to spend sampling the product at the end. You get three free samples of the beer as part of the tour.

Note that the Heineken Experience is immensely popular and queues start forming before it even opens. Visit is by tour only and there are a limited number of tours per day, each taking a limited number of people. If you don't get there early, you can face a very long wait or you may not get in at all. ❸ Stadhouderskade 78 ☎ 020 523 9666 ⓦ www.heinekenexperience.com ✉ info@heinekenexperience.com 🕐 11.00–19.00 June–Aug (last ticket sales 17.45); 10.00–18.00 Tues–Sun, Sept–May (last ticket sales 17.00) Ⓝ Tram: 16, 24, 25. Admission charge

city began a collection of herbal plants. The collection moved here in 1682 and it's a fabulous place to escape the city streets for a while. You could almost be transported to tropical Asia, from where many of the plants originally came, brought back by the Dutch East India Company from their trade expeditions to the Spice Islands and beyond.

The collection now ranges from the Arctic plants in the outdoor gardens to collections of orchids, cacti and palm trees in some of the greenhouses. There's a beautiful butterfly house too and an elevated walkway taking you through a rainforest canopy. ⓐ Plantage Middenlaan 2A ⓣ 020 625 9021 ⓕ 020 625 7006 ⓦ www.dehortus.nl ⓔ info@dehortus.nl ⓛ 09.00–17.00 Mon–Fri, 10.00–17.00 Sat & Sun, Feb–Nov; 10.00–17.00 Mon–Fri, 10.00–16.00 Sat & Sun, Dec–Jan ⓣ Tram: 6, 9, 14. Admission charge

Joods Historisch Museum (Jewish Historical Museum)

Some people think that Amsterdam's Jewish connection starts and ends with Anne Frank, but there was a reason the Frank family were hiding here. The city has a long Jewish history. This enterprising museum, which reveals this history, is housed in four converted synagogues that date back to the 17th and 18th centuries. The old alleyways and streets of the Jewish quarter have not been lost completely, but were used by the architects and cleverly incorporated into the building's design. Naturally, there is a big focus on the German occupation of the city, when an estimated 100,000 Jews were deported from here to the death camps. ⓐ Nieuwe Amstelstraat 1 ⓣ 020 531 0310 ⓕ 020 531 0311 ⓦ www.jhm.nl ⓔ info@jhm.nl ⓛ 11.00–17.00 Sun–Wed, 11.00–21.00 Thur ⓣ Tram: 9, 14. Admission charge

Magere Brug (Skinny Bridge)

The so-called Skinny Bridge is one of those sights in Amsterdam that's loved by locals and tourists alike. It is a simple but pretty bridge across the Amstel river that seems to sum up the look of the city. The current bridge dates back to 1670, but has been renovated since then. The story goes that it replaced an earlier and even skinnier bridge across the river, built by two sisters who lived on opposite

🔺 *Doing the up and under at Magere Brug*

sides and got tired of the long walk round whenever they wanted
to see each other. Their surname, allegedly, was *Magere*, meaning
'skinny'. It's a nice story, true or not, and even if you only spend five
minutes here taking the obligatory photo it's an essential image
of Amsterdam. ❸ Kerkstraat ⓥ Metro to Waterlooplein; Tram: 4

Scheepvaart Museum (Maritime Museum)
The story of how Amsterdam turned from a little fishing village into
the richest port in the world is wonderfully told in this maritime
museum, housed in what was once a naval dockyard. There is an
enjoyable film about the rise and fall of the Dutch East India Company

and at the front of the museum is a replica of a spice-trading ship. As you can see, the romance of the sea wasn't quite so romantic if you were below decks. The ship is a fully working replica and occasionally sets sail to visit other venues, so check if it's in port when you are. ⓐ Kattenburgerplein 1 ⓣ 020 523 2222 ⓕ 020 523 2329 ⓦ www.scheepvaartmuseum.nl ⓔ info@scheepvaartmuseum.nl ⓛ 10.00–17.00 Tues–Sun; also open Mon, mid-June to mid-Sept ⓜ Metro to Centraal Station; Bus: 22, 32. Admission charge

CULTURE

Foam

A centre for independent and contemporary photography and documentary, this small museum of all things photographic has put Amsterdam on the international map. Covering exhibits from well-known photographers to emerging talent, you can easily lose hours in a good exhibition. ⓐ Keizersgracht 609 ⓣ 020 551 6500 ⓦ www.foam.nl ⓛ 10.00–18.00 Sat–Wed, 10.00–21.00 Thur & Fri ⓜ Tram: 16, 24, 25 to Keizersgracht. Admission charge

Museum Van Loon

This late 17th-century canal house was owned from 1884–1945 by the Van Loon family, one of whose ancestors was a founder of the Dutch East India Company. Although Willem van Loon didn't live here at the time, it gives a good impression of what a rich merchant's life would have been like. The opulence of the rooms and the furniture, the marble staircase and the huge collection of family portraits all paint a picture of a life of luxury and privilege. It's a rare chance to look into one of these grand canal homes. Don't forget to check out the garden as well. ⓐ Keizersgracht 672 ⓣ 020 624 5255 ⓕ 020 427 4124

ⓦ www.museumvanloon.nl ⓔ info@museumvanloon.nl
🕐 11.00–17.00 Wed–Mon ⓝ Tram: 16, 24, 25. Admission charge

Tropenmuseum (Tropical Museum)
A study of the tropical regions of the world is an unusual theme for a museum in the Netherlands, you might think, but don't forget the Dutch have long had links with, and even ruled, tropical places such as Suriname, Indonesia and several Caribbean islands. The museum sprang out of that history but now takes in the rest of the tropical world. You can walk through an Arab souk and an African village as well as learn about the spice trade. The 19th-century building looks imposing from the outside, but the interior is cleverly designed to include lots of light and space. If you're with children, don't miss the Tropenmuseum Junior or Kindermuseum (Children's Museum).
ⓐ Linnaeusstraat 2 ⓣ 020 568 8200 ⓕ 020 668 4579
ⓦ www.tropenmuseum.nl ⓔ tropenmuseum@kit.nl 🕐 10.00–17.00
ⓝ Bus: 22; Tram: 9. Admission charge

Verzetsmuseum (Dutch Resistance Museum)
If you tour the Anne Frank House in Amsterdam – and most first-time city visitors do – you should also visit the Resistance Museum. It is equally moving and helps to paint the broader picture of what happened in the city during the Nazi occupation from 1940 to 1945. Amsterdam had by far the biggest Jewish community in the Netherlands and experienced some of the greatest suffering. Anne Frank was just one of thousands of people hidden from the Germans by Amsterdam's brave citizens, who risked their own lives in order to save others. It is their story that is told here, including those people who survived, and those who didn't. ⓐ Plantage Kerklaan 61 ⓣ 020 620 2535
ⓦ www.verzetsmuseum.org ⓔ info@verzetsmuseum.org

🕐 10.00–17.00 Tues–Fri, 12.00–17.00 Sat–Mon 🚊 Tram: 6, 20.
Admission charge

RETAIL THERAPY

Markets

This is a terrific area for markets. If visiting the Oosterpark or Artis Zoo, take a detour to the **Dappermarkt** (📍 Dapperstraat 🕐 Mon–Sat). At one end it's a general street market comprising mainly clothes stalls. Further on it turns into a food market with lots of ethnic produce. It's colourful and lively and lots of food shops line the same street.

In the very southern end of this quarter of the city, beyond the Heineken Experience, the district known as De Pijp has one of the biggest and best street markets in the city. The **Albert Cuypmarkt** (🌐 www.albertcuypmarkt.com 🕐 Mon–Sat 🚊 Tram: 4 to Stadhouderskade; Tram: 16, 24, 25 to Albert Cuypstraat) sprawls over several streets and sells clothes, general household goods and food from all over the world, reflecting the multicultural make-up of Amsterdam.

There's also the **Waterlooplein Flea Market** (🕐 10.00–17.00 Mon–Sat 🚇 Metro: 51, 53, 54 to Waterlooplein), alongside the Amstel very close to the Rembrandt House Museum. Here you can buy souvenirs, CDs, paintings, antiques, funky clothes and jewellery, not to mention second-hand clothes and bric-a-brac.

Finally there's the **Bloemenmarkt (Flower Market** 📍 Muntplein 🕐 09.30–17.00 Mon–Sat, 12.00–17.00 Sun 🚊 Tram: 9, 16 to Muntplein). If you want tulips from Amsterdam, this is the place to get them, along with a wide range of other blooms from the fertile flower-growing fields of the Netherlands. Even if you don't buy, it makes a great photo opportunity.

TAKING A BREAK

De Taart van m'n Tante £ ❶ A kitsch café serving stylish *ooh la la* cakes, this little place is full of locals eagerly sinking their teeth into colourful confectionery. ⓐ Ferdinand Bolstraat 10 ⓣ 020 776 4600 ⓦ www.detaart.nl ⓛ 10.00–18.00 ⓝ Tram: 16, 25 to Ferdinand Bolstraat

Café Kanis & Meiland £–££ ❷ This excellent *eetcafé* in the redeveloped dockland to the east of Centraal Station is a mix of bar and restaurant, with a lovely terrace overlooking the water. ⓐ Levantkade 127 ⓣ 020 418 2439 ⓛ 10.00–01.00 Sun–Thur, 10.00–03.00 Fri & Sat, kitchen open 10.00–22.00 ⓝ Bus: 32 to KNSM Eiland

De Odessa £–££ ❸ Enjoy the novelty factor of eating on a Ukrainian fishing boat. Moored behind a shopping centre in Amsterdam's docks, the Odessa is quirky and hip, with DJs spinning after 22.00 and food and drinks served most of the day. ⓐ Veemkade 259 ⓣ 020 419 3010 ⓛ 11.00–01.00 Sun–Thur, 11.00–03.00 Fri & Sat ⓝ Tram: 26 to Rietlandpark

AFTER DARK

RESTAURANTS

Badcuyp £ ❹ A centre for live world music, Badcuyp boasts an organic *eetcafé* with friendly staff, healthy, delicious food and a pleasant atmosphere. ⓐ Eerste Sweelinckstraat 10 ⓣ 020 675 9669 ⓕ 020 670 8913 ⓦ www.badcuyp.nl ⓛ 11.00–15.00 & 17.30–21.30 Mon–Sat, 13.00–15.00 & 17.30–21.30 Sun ⓝ Tram: 4, 16, 24, 25

Cambodja City £ ❺ Fantastic range of dishes from Thailand, Vietnam and Cambodia. Also does takeaways. ⓐ Albert Cuypstraat 58–60

🕿 020 671 4930 🕘 17.00–22.00 Tues–Sun ⓝ Tram: 4, 16, 24, 25 to Albert Cuypstraat

Kilimanjaro £–££ ❻ This long-standing African restaurant has some unusual dishes, including antelope and crocodile, but vegetarians have plenty of choice too. ⓐ Rapenburgerplein 6 🕿 020 622 3485 🕘 17.00–22.00 Tues–Sun ⓝ Bus: 22; Tram: 7, 9

Girassol ££ ❼ Friendly, family-run Portuguese restaurant with a terrace overlooking the Amstel. Good fresh fish and a reasonably priced wine list, this is a treat for a sunny day. ⓐ Weesperzijde 135 🕿 020 692 3471 ⓦ www.girassol.nl 🕘 12.00–15.00 & 18.00–22.00 Mon–Fri, 18.00–22.00 Sat & Sun ⓝ Metro: 51, 53, 54 to Wibausstraat

🔺 *There's plenty of choice when you need a break from sightseeing*

Olive & Cookie ££ ❽ An intimate restaurant that gives vegetarians a good name. Friendly, affordable and with great service to match its food. ⓐ Saenreamstraat 67 ⓣ 020 470 7190 ⓛ 13.00–21.00 Mon–Sat ⓝ Tram: 16, 24, 25 to Weteringsplantsoen

Fifteen ££–£££ ❾ Jamie Oliver's Dutch outpost offers exceptional food, great service and a top-notch waterfront location. ⓐ Jollemanhof 9 ⓣ 0900 343 8336 ⓦ www.fifteen.nl ⓛ 12.00–15.00 & 18.00–01.00, kitchen open until 23.00 ⓝ Tram: 26 towards IJburg

Mamouche ££–£££ ❿ North African couscous, lamb and fish tagine dishes. Reservations are a must. ⓐ Quellynstraat 104 ⓣ 020 673 6361 ⓦ www.restaurantmamouche.nl ⓛ 18.00–23.00 ⓝ Tram: 16, 24, 25 to Weteringsplantsoen

De Kas £££ ⓫ Some of the finest food in the city, served either in the spacious dining room (formerly a greenhouse) or outdoors next to the herb gardens. ⓐ Kamerlingh Onneslaan 3 ⓣ 020 462 4562 ⓦ www.restaurantdekas.nl ⓛ 12.00–14.00 Mon–Fri, 18.30–22.00 Mon–Sat ⓝ Tram: 9 to Hogeweg; Bus: 59, 69, 169

La Rive £££ ⓬ Arguably the best restaurant in the city, with 2 Michelin stars and prices to match. ⓐ Amstel Intercontinental Hotel, Professor Tulpplein 1 ⓣ 020 520 3264 ⓦ www.restaurantlarive.com ⓛ 12.00–14.00 & 18.30–22.30 Mon–Fri, 18.30–22.30 Sat ⓝ Tram: 7, 10 to Sarphatistraat

BARS & CLUBS

There's no lack of clubs in this area and with the docks being developed new ones spring up constantly. Ask around or look for flyers.

Brouwerij 't Ij Look for the windmill to find this microbrewery with its no frills (and no food) tasting room and roof terrace.
🅐 Funenkade 7 ☎ 020 622 8325 🆆 www.brouwerijhetij.nl
🕑 15.00–20.00 Wed–Sun Ⓝ Tram: 10; Bus: 22

Café de Druif This cosy, atmospheric brown café has watched boats and people come and go since 1631. 🅐 Rapenburgerplein 83
☎ 020 624 4530 🕑 11.00–01.00 Sun–Thur, 11.00–02.00 Fri & Sat
Ⓝ Metro: 51, 53, 54 to Nieuwmarkt

Escape Amsterdam's largest venue, the Escape can accommodate a few thousand clubbers each night. The regular Saturday Framebusters is a huge draw, as well as Sundae's (naturally on Sundays) with its Ibiza vibe. Dress smart. 🅐 Rembrandtplein 11 ☎ 020 622 1111
🆆 www.escape.nl 🕑 23.00–04.00 Thur, 23.00–05.00 Fri & Sat, 23.00–04.30 Sun Ⓝ Tram: 4, 9, 20 to Rembrandtplein

⬤ Chill out with the locals in a brown bar

Museumplein (Museum Quarter)

Sooner or later, every visitor to Amsterdam makes it to what's popularly known as the Museum Quarter, the area surrounding the huge Museumplein square.

On the square itself you'll find the big two attractions, the Rijksmuseum and the Van Gogh Museum, although the Rijksmuseum is currently being renovated and is only partially open to the public until work is completed. The lesser-known but important Stedelijk Modern Art Museum is also under construction and has temporarily been rehoused in the Post CS building near Centraal Station. Close by is one of the slickest diamond factory tours at Coster Diamonds, as well as the hugely popular Vondelpark, one of the biggest green spaces within easy reach of the city centre.

The Museum Quarter itself is also an interesting part of the city, more than just a place where museums happen to be. The tunnel that splits the Rijksmuseum in two had a major road running through it until as recently as the 1990s. Then the square, Amsterdam's largest, was turned into a miniature park and while it still has the feel of an artificially made place, it's much more pleasant than it used to be. At one corner, you'll find a small area for skateboarders and at the far end, people like to congregate on the roof of supermarket Albert Hein, which was built into a man-made hill. It is often used for huge celebrations or demonstrations.

SIGHTS & ATTRACTIONS

Coster Diamonds

This is one of the busier of Amsterdam's diamond factories, thanks to its proximity to the two main museums and to its coach parking

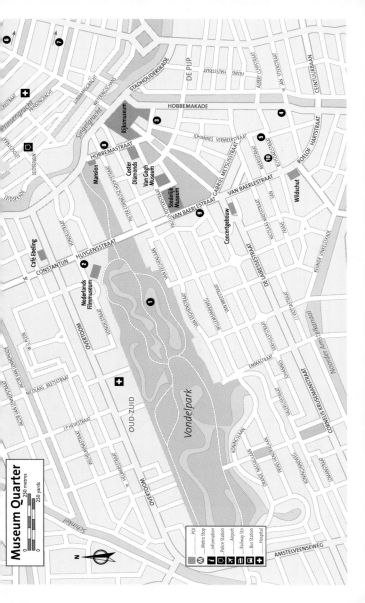

Museum Quarter

0 ___ 250 metres
0 ___ 250 yards

Legend:
- POI
- Metro Stop
- Information
- Police Station
- Airport
- Railway Stn
- Bus Station
- Hospital

N

Labels on map

Schinkel

Prinsengracht

KNSTRAAT

PRINSENGRACHT

LIJNBAANSGRACHT

WETERINGSCHANS

STADHOUDERSKADE

DE PIJP

HOBBEMAKADE

FRANS HALSSTRAAT

ALBERT CUYPSTRAAT

CEINTUURBAAN

'er VAN STEENSTRAAT

Singelgracht

LEIDSEKADE

LEIDSEBOSJE

Café Eeling

CONSTANTIJN HUYGENSSTRAAT

Nederlands Filmmuseum

HOBBEMASTRAAT

JOHANNES VERMEERSTRAAT

GABRIEL METSUSTRAAT

ROELOF HARTSTRAAT

Mansion

Coster Diamonds

Van Gogh Museum

Stedelijk Museum

PETER CORNELISZ HOOFTSTRAAT

PAULUS POTTERSTRAAT

'S VAN BAERLESTRAAT

VAN BAERLESTRAAT

Concertgebouw

Wildschut

VONDELSTRAAT

VAN EEGHENLAAN

VAN EEGHENSTRAAT

WILLEMSPARKWEG

VAN BREESTRAAT

JAN LUIJKENSTRAAT

OVERTOOM

OUD-ZUID

W.G. PLEIN

NICOLAAS BEETSSTRAAT

JACOB VAN LENNEPKADE

J.F. HEIJESTRAAT

WILHELMINASTRAAT

1e HELMERSSTRAAT

OVERTOOM

Vondelpark

KONINGSLAAN

ORANJE NASSAULAAN

KONINGINNEWEG

CORNELIS KRUSEMANSTRAAT

CORNELIS SCHUYTSTRAAT

EMMASTRAAT

DE LAIRESSESTRAAT

NICOLAAS MAESSTRAAT

FRANS VAN MIERISSTRAAT

REIJNIER VINKELESKADE

Noorder Amstelkanaal

AMSTELVEENSEWEG

Rijksmuseum

1 2 3 4 5 6 7 8 9 10

facilities. Coach groups do get the attention of the tour guides and individual visitors might find themselves squeezed out or waiting longer than usual for the next tour to start, so if you see several coaches lined up outside it may be best to come back at another time. Free tours run roughly every half hour in summer (hourly in winter), although this varies depending on availability of guides for the different languages catered for.

The tour teaches you a bit about the diamond trade and its history and explains why Amsterdam is one of the world's main diamond centres after Antwerp. You can watch diamonds being

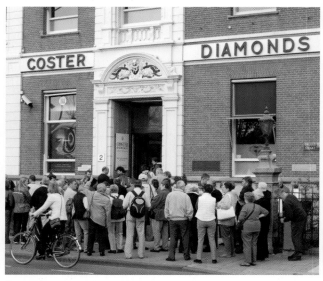

🔺 *Find out about Amsterdam's diamond trade at Coster Diamonds*

polished, learn the grades that exist and discover why some stones cost more than others. You can also see the skilled cutters and polishers perfecting the raw material, known as the 'rough'. At the end you're given a close encounter with diamonds and jewellery and, of course, a chance to buy. **ⓐ** Paulus Potterstraat 2–8 **ⓘ** 020 305 5555 **ⓦ** www.costerdiamonds.com **ⓔ** info@costerdiamonds.com **ⓛ** 09.00–17.00 **Ⓝ** Tram: 2, 5, 20

Vondelpark

Amsterdammers are exceedingly fond of the Vondelpark and make full use of its 45 hectares (111 acres) all year round and especially in summer. More than eight million people visit the park every year, which has been providing green relief to the city dwellers ever since it opened in 1865. The park is the biggest in the city and is filled with trees, pathways, ponds and lakes teeming with wildlife, children's playgrounds, a bandstand, a rose garden and the **Nederlands Filmmuseum** (**ⓘ** 020 589 1400 **ⓦ** www.filmmuseum.nl). There are occasional concerts put on during the summer, in the bandstand.

The park is named after Joost van den Vondel, a popular Dutch poet who lived from 1587–1679. Originally it was only 4 hectares (10 acres), designed in the then-fashionable English style for city parks. It proved so popular it was extended to its present size in 1877.

The Filmmuseum, which is an archive and a good place to hang out as well as a museum, sometimes hosts free outdoor films on a summer Saturday night. The rest of the year it shows films of all kinds, in the original language, from Charlie Chaplin through to the latest releases. If you can't speak the language or read Dutch subtitles, then it's probably better to have a coffee downstairs at restaurant Vertigo. **ⓐ** Information Centre: Vondelstraat 69 **ⓛ** Dawn to dusk **Ⓝ** Tram: 1, 2, 3, 5, 6, 10, 17 to Leidseplein; Museumboat

CULTURE

Concertgebouw (Concert Theatre)

The Concert Theatre is worth a look even if you don't enjoy classical music. It has been the home of the Royal Concertgebouw Orchestra since 1888 and in that time some great names including Mahler, Ravel and Richard Strauss have conducted here. The building has some of the best acoustics in the world and if you fancy a concert, check the website or call in for details. The Concert Hall tries to be accessible to everyone, offering inexpensive concerts on Sunday mornings and Saturday matinees. There is also often a summer series of cheaper performances. There are two halls inside. Try to get a ticket for the main *Grote Zaal* (Great Hall) if you can, rather than the *Kleine Zaal* (Small Hall or Recital Hall).
ⓐ Concertgebouwplein 2–6 ① 020 671 8345 ⓦ www.concertgebouw.nl

Rijksmuseum

The Rijksmuseum is the major national art gallery of the Netherlands. The grand building, which opened in 1885, was designed by Petrus Josephus Hubertus Cuypers, the architect who produced Centraal Station. A lengthy refurbishment means that much of the museum is closed to the public until at least the summer of 2008.. This is no reason not to visit now, however, as the highlights of the collection have been kept on display in 13 rooms in the Philips Wing, to the rear of the building. In some ways this is even better than visiting the whole museum, as you'll see the best exhibits gathered together in the same space – a truly rich collection.

In one room currently open to the public you can admire 17 of the museum's works by Rembrandt. The most important work in the Rijksmuseum, Rembrandt's *The Nightwatch*, is displayed in a separate room. This monumental canvas is so huge and powerful that it will stop you in your tracks. Some of Rembrandt's self-portraits, showing him moving from youth to old age, are among the finest ever painted. In some you expect him to move, to breathe or to start a conversation. A visit here, as well as to the Rembrandt House Museum (see page 70) will give you a unique insight into the artist and his work.

The other great Dutch name in the collection is Vermeer, whose works are also kept available in this temporary display. The most well-known is *The Kitchen Maid*, a beautifully lit portrait of a young woman pouring milk into a bowl. Other Dutch masters whose works can be seen include Jan Steen and Frans Hals. On display you'll find some fine arts items alongside the old masters, including some wonderful delftware porcelain. ⓐ Jan Luijkenstraat 1 ⓣ 020 674 7000 ⓕ 020 674 7001 ⓦ www.rijksmuseum.nl ⓔ info@rijksmuseum.nl ⓛ 09.00–18.00, Sat–Thur, 09.00–22.00 Fri ⓝ Tram: 2, 5; Museumboat. Admission charge

▲ *The Rijksmuseum is one of the world's great art galleries*

VAN GOGH MUSEUM

The Van Gogh Museum is the single most visited attraction in Amsterdam. This isn't surprising as it is a delightful museum featuring the finest collection of works by one of the world's best-known artists. It contains about 200 paintings, almost 600 drawings and 700 original letters, mostly written by Vincent Van Gogh to his brother Theo. There's also a collection of works by contemporaries of Van Gogh and by people who influenced him or were influenced by him. Names here include Toulouse-Lautrec, Monet, Pissarro and Gaugin, who lived with Van Gogh in France for two months.

The artist's self-portraits are arguably the most striking exhibits. He stares out of the canvas at you unflinchingly and with several portraits displayed side by side it's an unnerving experience to look back at them. One display shows the oriental work that influenced Van Gogh and hints at the sensitive and delicate side of this mad, misunderstood genius.

There are four floors altogether plus an annexe. The collection is so large that some of the minor works, such as the drawings, are displayed on a rotating basis. There are also temporary exhibitions. The main attractions, which include popular paintings such as *Wheatfield with Crows*, *The Potato Eaters*, *The Yellow House* and one of the *Sunflowers* paintings, are usually on display unless a special exhibition sees them out on loan.

Allow time to visit the excellent museum shop. Posters are especially popular and come in distinctive triangular cartons that you see people carrying all over the city. You can find some tasteful souvenirs, stationery and books, or you can pick up novelty items such as Van Gogh fridge magnets.

The building is light, airy and spacious, which does help it to cope well with its many visitors. If you don't like crowds, however, try to get there 15–20 minutes before the doors open or for the last hour or so in the day, though you should still allow plenty of time to see everything before it closes. Visiting at less busy times of year, such as in the winter, is also recommended.

ⓐ Paulus Potterstraat 7 ⓣ 020 570 5200 ⓕ 020 570 5222 ⓦ www.vangoghmuseum.nl ⓔ info@vangoghmuseum.nl ⓛ 10.00–18.00 Sat–Thur, 10.00–22.00 Fri ⓝ Tram: 2, 5; Museumboat. Admission charge

● The jolly Van Gogh Museum bus

Stedelijk Museum

The current home of the city's modern art museum, which focuses on art from the late 19th century onwards, is not actually in the Museum Quarter but over near Centraal Station. The actual site is being refurbished and is scheduled to open some time in 2008. Until then the temporary home is called Stedelijk CS, to distinguish it from the core collection.

At the Stedelijk CS base you will find a small part of the main collection, along with temporary exhibitions of modern art which typify the often provocative nature of the work in the museum's core collection. There are some great names here, interestingly often represented by lesser-known works. The Stedelijk has three Van Goghs along with works by Picasso, Renoir and Cézanne, Andy Warhol and Willem de Kooning.

Temporary exhibitions range from photography and video installations through to multimedia works, from the brilliant to the obscure.

Stedelijk CS ⓐ Oosterdokskade 5 Ⓝ Metro to Centraal Station; Tram: 1, 2, 4, 5, 6, 9, 13, 16, 17, 24, 25

Stedelijk Museum (2008 onwards) ⓐ Paulus Potterstraat 13
ⓣ 020 573 2911 ⓕ 020 675 2716 Ⓦ www.stedelijk.nl ⓔ info@stedelijk.nl
🕐 10.00–18.00 Ⓝ Tram: 2, 5, 20; Museumboat. Admission charge

RETAIL THERAPY

Pieter Cornelisz Hooftstraat On this swish street between the Museumplein and the entrance to the Vondelpark you'll find some of the most expensive shopping in the city. Names like Gucci, Armani, Versace, Cartier and Louis Vuitton rub shoulders with the best Dutch designers, surrounded by some smart cafés and restaurants.
Ⓝ Tram: 1, 2, 5, 6, 10, 17 to Leidseplein

Van Gogh Museum Shop Only accessible from the museum, and not to be confused with the separate shop that's halfway between here and the Rijksmuseum (though this too is excellent), the Van Gogh Museum Shop has one of the best selections in the city for either yourself or friends of an artistic frame of mind. Posters are popular but only the start of it. ⓐ Paulus Potterstraat 7 ⓣ 020 570 5200 ⓕ 020 570 5222 ⓦ www.vangoghmuseum.nl ⓛ 10.00–18.00 Sat–Thur, 10.00–22.00 Fri ⓝ Tram: 2, 5; Museumboat

TAKING A BREAK

With the renovation of both the Rijksmuseum and the Stedelijk, the Van Gogh Museum is the only one that currently has a working restaurant – and very good it is too, with snacks and drinks available all day, hot meals at lunchtime and a special dinner on a Friday evening when the museum stays open late.

't Blauwe Theehuis £ ❶ You'll find this lovely 1930s café in the Vondelpark. It has a large terrace and serves food from breakfast onwards. Upstairs, there's a smarter, if tiny, bar and restaurant with DJs some weekend evenings. ⓐ Vondelpark 5 ⓣ 020 662 0254 ⓦ www.blauwetheehuis.nl ⓛ 09.00–23.00

Café Vertigo £ ❷ This terrific place is next to the Filmmuseum, overlooking the Vondelpark. It's ideal for a snack and a drink outside on sultry nights, or for a romantic candlelit dinner. Menus change according to the films being shown at the museum, so expect anything from Hollywood to Bollywood. ⓐ Vondelpark 3 ⓣ 020 612 3021 ⓦ www.vertigo.nl ⓛ 10.00–01.00

101

Cobra Café £ ❸ Right on the Museumsplein, this newish place is named after the CoBrA expressionist art movement – and the striking décor reflects this. It has floor-to-ceiling glass walls, giving you good views across the square and the street entertainers in the area. The food is simple but the atmosphere is relaxing. ⓐ Hobbemastraat 18 ❶ 020 470 0111 ⓦ www.cobracafe.com ⓛ 10.00–22.00 ⓝ Tram: 2, 5 to Museumsplein; Museumboat

AFTER DARK

RESTAURANTS

Pheun Thai £ ❹ As usual, if you want a good, cheap meal in a pricier part of the city look to the ethnic restaurants. This is more like a café but the food is fabulous. Also sells takeaway. ⓐ Hobbemakade 71 ❶ 020 427 4537 ⓛ 17.00–22.00 ⓝ Tram: 5

Eetcafé Loetje £–££ ❺ This steakhouse/bar is very close to the Museumplein and is well worth seeking out. Often packed and always buzzing, it serves daily specials and has a conservatory restaurant. ⓐ Johannes Vermeerstraat 52 ❶ 020 662 8173 ⓛ 11.00–23.00 Mon–Sat, kitchen closed Sat lunch ⓝ Tram: 16

Kitsch £–££ ❻ True to its name, this hip little place is full of atmosphere. The menu is amusing but good, with healthy portions and great value for money. Only go if you can handle disco, ABBA or dated MTV videos running in the background. ⓐ Utrechtsestraat 42 ❶ 020 625 9251 ⓛ 18.00–23.00 Mon–Thur, 18.00–00.00 Fri & Sat, Sept–July; 18.00–23.00 Wed & Thur, 18.00–00.00 Fri & Sat, Aug ⓝ Bus: 4; Metro to Waterlooplein; Tram: 4 to Utrechtsestraat

🔺 *Amsterdammers relaxing in the Vondelpark*

Pata Negra £–££ ❼ A bustling tapas bar, this place serves great sangria – and tapas, once they arrive. Come here if you're looking for good food and a lively night out, but be warned that the busier it gets, the more chaotic the service. ⓐ Utrechtsestraat 124 ❶ 020 422 6250 ⓒ 14.00–23.30 ⓝ Tram: 4 to Utrechtsestraat

Sama Sebo ££ ❽ Allegedly the best Indonesian restaurant in town. Go for the 20-dish *rijsttafel*, or pick a pavement table in summer for people-watching on the most fashionable shopping street in the city. ⓐ PC Hooftstraat 27 ❶ 020 662 8146 ⓒ 12.00–15.00 & 18.00–22.00 Mon–Sat ⓝ Tram: 1, 2, 5, 6, 10, 17 to Leidseplein

Bodega Keyzer ££–£££ If you want an old-fashioned Dutch restaurant, formal and grand with waiters dressed as they were when the place opened in 1905, then the Keyzer is it. You can eat more cheaply in the more casual café at the front, but be prepared to shell out if you book the restaurant. ⓐ Van Baerlestraat 96 ⓣ 020 675 1866 ⓛ 09.00–24.00 Mon–Sat, 11.00–24.00 Sun ⓝ Tram: 2 to Willemsparkweg; Tram: 3, 5, 12 to Van Baerlestraat; Tram: 16 to De Lairessestraat

Le Garage £££ Definitely the place for a blow-out treat, Le Garage is as fashionable as it gets in Amsterdam. It is a huge converted garage, with mirrored walls and tables and attracts a smart crowd who pack out the tables tightly wedged against each other. It's a place to dress up for, though if you want to go more casual there's an annexe called Le Garage en Pluche serving Indonesian-style street food. ⓐ Ruysdaelstraat 54–56 ⓣ 020 679 7176 ⓛ 12.00–14.00 & 18.00–23.00 Mon–Fri, 18.00–23.00 Sat & Sun ⓝ Tram: 3, 5, 12, 24 to Roelof Hartplein

BARS & CLUBS

Café Ebeling In Amsterdam, where people go to a coffee house for something rather stronger than coffee, a café is often what the rest of the world would call a bar. Café Ebeling, set up in an old bank building with the toilets in the vaults, is one of these. There are sofas to lounge on and a drinks menu which covers everything from draught Guinness to wine by the glass. It's a great late-night hang-out if you don't fancy a club or disco. ⓐ Overtoom 50 ⓣ 020 689 4858 ⓦ www.cafeebeling.com ⓛ 11.00–01.00 Mon–Thur, 11.00–03.00 Fri & Sat, 12.00–01.00 Sun ⓝ Tram: 1, 17

MUSEUMPLEIN (MUSEUM QUARTER)

Mansion A fusion of club, bar and restaurant. The top floor serves modern Chinese cuisine. Below are several bars for lounging in; the ground floor is strictly for dancing. ⓐ Hobbemastraat 2 ⓣ 020 616 6664 ⓦ www.the-mansion.nl ⓛ Restaurant 18.00–23.00 Mon–Sat, Bar 18.00–01.00 Mon–Thur, 18.00–03.00 Fri & Sat, Club 21.00–03.00 Fri & Sat ⓝ Tram: 2, 5 to Hobbemastraat

OCCII This one-time squat at the far end of the Vondelpark has been turned into an alternative venue typical of Amsterdam, with cabaret, theatre and non-mainstream music. ⓐ Amstelveenseweg 134 ⓣ 020 671 7778 ⓦ www.occii.org ⓛ 21.30–02.00 Sun–Thur, 21.30–03.00 Fri & Sat ⓝ Tram: 1, 2 to Amstelveenseweg

Paradiso This is mostly a live music venue, but also hosts club nights with top international DJs and special events. Housed in a former church, it has become an Amsterdam institution and is the city's premier music venue, showcasing 700 artists a year. ⓐ Weteringschans 6 ⓣ 020 626 4521 ⓦ www.paradiso.nl ⓛ Times vary ⓝ Tram: 1, 2, 5, 7, 10 to Leidseplein

Wildschut This grand art deco café bar is on a square of equally grand buildings, with a terrace enabling you to enjoy them as Amsterdammers have done for more than 80 years. It's often difficult to get a table in summer, because it's always jammed with everyone from bohemians to businessmen. On cold evenings the inside is cosy, with some intimate little booths where you can enjoy a simple meal. Snacks and drinks are served all day, but it's a terrific spot for a nightcap and is popular with audiences from the Concert Hall a few blocks away. ⓐ Roelof Hartplein 1–3 ⓣ 020 673 8622 ⓛ 09.00–0.100 Mon–Fri, 10.00–late Sat & Sun ⓝ Tram: 3, 5, 12, 20, 24 to Roelof Hartplein

105

THE CITY

Western Canal Ring

This area west of the city centre has everything from the brash Leidseplein, a Dutch version of London's Leicester Square or New York's Times Square, through to the picturesque canals of the Jordaan district. On the edge of the Jordaan is one of the city's major attractions, the Anne Frank House.

The Jordaan, which makes up the northern end of this district, used to be a working-class neighbourhood. It then became a bohemian hangout and has subsequently turned into one of the most fashionable areas of the city to live. It hasn't lost its bohemian feel, though, and its pretty appearance makes it very popular with visitors. There are tree-lined canals, brown bars and cafés, quirky shops, people cycling through the streets and photo opportunities galore. It's a great place to stay and there's a good choice of accommodation from the cheap to the chic, from the old to the new. There are plenty of eating places, too, covering all budgets. The nightlife around the Jordaan district tends to consist of a long, leisurely meal or late-night drinks in a neighbourhood bar. If you want nightclub action, head south to the Leidseplein.

SIGHTS & ATTRACTIONS

Anne Frank Huis

Visiting the house where Anne Frank wrote her famous teenage diaries is one of the most moving of all Amsterdam experiences. The building itself is an old merchant's house, built in 1635. It wasn't designed to cope with the huge numbers of visitors that come today and because some of the rooms are small with narrow stairways, a visit can be slow-moving. Try to be there before it opens to miss the crowds and queues.

Western Canal Ring

0   250 metres
0   250 yards

WILLEMSSTRAAT

Brouwersgracht

NIEUWE WESTERDOKSTRAAT

LINDENGRACHT

HAARLEMMERSTRAAT

NOORDER-MARKT

JORDAAN

WESTERSTRAAT

TUINSTRAAT

EGELANTIERSGRACHT

Egelantiersgracht

Anne Frank Huis

Westerkerk

Theatermuseum

RAADHUISSTRAAT

DAM SQUARE

OUD STAD

CENTRUM

ROZENGRACHT

ROZENSTRAAT

LAURIERSTRAAT

Lauriergracht

ELANDSTRAAT

Wolvenstraat 23

ELANDSGRACHT

Amsterdams Historisch Museum

RUNSTRAAT

Universiteit van Amsterdam

Allard Pierson Museum

LOOIERSGRACHT

LOOIERSGRACHT

Singel

SINGEL

AMSTEL

Leidsegracht

Herengracht

Herengracht

LEIDSESTRAAT

KERKSTRAAT

HERENGRACHT

VIJZELGRACHT

LEIDSEPLEIN

Prinsengracht

STADHOUDERSKADE

WETERINGSCHANS

Rijksmuseum

OVERTOOM

VONDELSTRAAT

P C HOOFTSTRAAT

CONSTANTIJN HUYGENSSTRAAT

NASSAUKADE

NASSAUKADE

MARNIXSTRAAT

LIJNBAANSGRACHT

Singelgracht

Bloemgracht

Prinsengracht

Keizersgracht

Herengracht

Singel

NIEUWEZIJDS VOORBURGWAL

NIEUWENDIJK

DAMRAK

WARMOESSTRAAT

OUDEZIJDS VOORBURGWAL

ROKIN

KALVERSTRAAT

VIJZELSTRAAT

N.SPIEGELSTRAAT

POI
M Metro Stop
i Information
Police Station
Airport
Railway Stn
Bus Station
Hospital

ANNE FRANK

Anne Frank was a Jewish girl unlucky enough to live in the Netherlands during the German occupation of World War II. Born in 1929, she died tragically young in March 1945 in the Nazi death camp at Belsen.

The Frank family had come to Amsterdam from Frankfurt in Germany when Adolf Hitler came to power in 1933. Anne's father Otto Frank began to build up two businesses in the city, one selling herbs and spices and the other producing pectin for jam. Seven years later Hitler invaded the Netherlands. When Anne's sister Margot was called to go to a so-called work project in Germany – in effect a death sentence – Otto Frank took his family into hiding in the tiny rooms above his business premises. They stayed there, crammed together in virtual secrecy, for 25 months. Eventually, they were betrayed to the authorities.

The diary that Anne Frank kept of the family's secret life became an international bestseller and brings millions of people to see the old merchant's house in which she lived. The diary speaks for itself. If you can, read Anne Frank's diary just before visiting to get the full emotional impact. You'll probably want to read it again afterwards, too, having seen the place where it was written.

The tour is self-guided and starts with some background exhibitions moving through to the original part of the house where Otto Frank had his business.

◀ *The Anne Frank Huis – an ordinary façade hides an extraordinary story*

You visit the offices above the workshops, then head up to the annexe where the Frank family lived. It is tiny and has you shaking your head in wonder that eight people could have lived here for over two years almost without detection.

After visiting the secret annexe you move along to more exhibition areas, plus a library where you'll find a nice café to stop and reflect upon your visit. The rooms here have computer displays giving you more information on particular aspects of the house and of the whole Jewish experience during World War II. ❸ Prinsengracht 267 ❶ 020 556 7105 ❶ 020 620 7999 Ⓦ www.annefrank.nl ❸ info@annefrank.nl ❶ 09.00–21.00 Mar–Sept; 09.00–19.00 Oct–Feb, open until 22.00 Sat, July & Aug Ⓝ Tram: 13, 14, 17 to Westermarkt. Admission charge

The Jordaan district

The best way to visit the Jordaan district is to walk from Centraal Station. It is not too far, although heavy luggage might persuade you otherwise, and it's a great way to introduce yourself to the district.

After the bustle of the station concourse and modern city, the houses become older, quainter and smaller. This was once an overcrowded working-class slum and the size of the buildings along its narrow streets reflects this. Later renovated by an influx of students, artists and entrepreneurs, it's now perfectly picturesque. There are several bridges crossing the canals and in good weather you will see visitors and locals sitting outside the bars and cafés enjoying themselves. Jordaan is the kind of relaxed neighbourhood where you can live like a local. Stop off for a drink, find a favourite spot and you may never want to leave.

You might find yourself checking the prices of some of the impressive old canal-side houses, whose tall, elegant lines make the district so attractive. You might wonder what it's like to live on

◆ *Relax over a drink in the Jordaan District*

a canal boat, as some people do. Or you might look enviously at one of the old alms houses dotted around the district. These homes, called *hofjes*, can be found in courtyards glimpsed from the main streets. Feel free to take a look round, though always remember they are people's homes and not tourist attractions. For a good example of a *hofje* that dates back to 1626, try to find the strangely named **Claes Claesz Hofje** on Egelantiersstraat (nos 34–54). Claes Claesz was the name of the merchant who founded it.

There are some nice churches here, too, notably the Westerkerk (see page 113), and some fun markets. However, the Jordaan is above all a place for pleasurable strolling and losing yourself in the cosy atmosphere. Here you can find your own personal piece of Amsterdam.

Leidseplein

There couldn't be more of a contrast to some of the quieter parts of the Jordaan than the brash, busy, neon-lit Leidseplein. It is only neon-lit at night, of course, but that's when most people head for this square and the surrounding streets. They are packed with bars, cafés, restaurants, fast-food places, clubs, cinemas, souvenir shops and the weirdly wonderful art nouveau-style **American Hotel** (ⓐ Leidsekade 97 ❶ 020 556 3000 ⓦ www.amsterdamamerican.com). Take a look inside or at least have a drink in the café.

If you're not into nightlife there's not much to bring you here during the day except for the AUB Ticketshop (see page 28). This sells cheap last-minute tickets for the day's performances at many venues, as well as regular tickets for concerts and plays around the city. Otherwise, relax with a drink at one of the pavement cafés and watch the world go by – quite a show on Amsterdam's Leidseplein. Ⓝ Tram: 1, 2, 5, 6, 7, 10, 20; Museumboat

Westerkerk

The Dutch answer to London's Bow Bells is the Westerkerk and
many people only regard someone as a true Amsterdammer if they
grew up hearing its bells. It's the main church in the western part of
the city and its lofty tower is visible wherever there is a gap in the
tall canal-side buildings. Inside that tower is the heaviest bell in
Amsterdam – 7,500 kg (7.39 tons).

The Westerkerk was completed in 1631 and was one of the city's
first Protestant churches. It was kept deliberately plain as a reaction
to the Catholic inclination towards elaborate design, but is worth
visiting for its huge organ and its nave, which is the largest in
the Netherlands.

The other memorable thing about the church is that it's
where Rembrandt was buried in 1669. Don't waste your time
looking for his grave, as there isn't one – the artist's burial plot
was only rented and his bones were later moved to an unknown
location. You will find a plaque on the wall claiming to be the spot
where he was originally buried, but even this memorial omits the
name by which the artist was known, referring to him only as
R Harmensz Van Ryn.

Tower tours usually happen in summer only, every hour on
the hour when the church is open. It is an awkward climb as you
approach the top, but make it if you can. It's fascinating to see the
nooks and crannies hidden in the tower and at the top, 85 m (279 ft)
high, you get the pleasure of probably the finest view of the city.
Group tours can sometimes be booked outside of regular opening
times. ⓐ Prinsengracht 281 ⓣ 020 624 7766 ⓦ www.westerkerk.nl
ⓛ Church 11.00–15.00 Mon–Fri, Tower tours hourly 10.00–17.00
Mon–Fri, Apr–Sept. ⓝ Tram: 13, 14, 17, 20

CULTURE

Theatermuseum

On the lovely Herengracht canal in one of the finest 17th-century mansions in the city, the Theatermuseum is well worth a visit. Inside you can see some of the ornate decoration that was added to the house in the early 18th century, including a spiral staircase and painted ceilings. The museum extends into another lavish house next door. As well as its collection of costumes, props, old posters, photos and miniature theatres, the museum has an audio tour plus the chance to build your own stage design and produce sound effects. Children love it. ⓐ Herengracht 168 ❶ 020 551 3300 ❶ 020 551 3303 Ⓦ www.tin.nl ⓔ info@tin.nl ❶ 11.00–17.00 Mon–Fri, 13.00–17.00 Sat & Sun Ⓝ Tram: 13, 14, 17, 20

RETAIL THERAPY

Jordaan is a shopaholic's heaven. The streets are packed with specialist shops of all kinds selling antiques, cheese, books, tea, coffee, shoes, jewellery, buttons and more. **De Witte Tandenwinkel** (White Teeth Shop ⓐ Runstraat 5) sells anything and everything to do with teeth, including children's toothbrushes.

In addition there are several markets, with stalls offering anything from conventional fruit and vegetables to bric-a-brac. Head for the **Noordermarkt** in the Jordaan district (ⓐ Boomstraat, just off Prinsengracht ❶ 09.00–13.00 Mon Ⓝ Tram: 3, 10) for antiques, books, CDs and clothes. The same area on a Saturday hosts an excellent organic food market (❶ 09.00–16.00). There's more junk on offer in the indoor **Rommelmarkt** (**Rummage Market** ⓐ Looiersgracht 38 ❶ 11.00–17.00 Ⓝ Tram: 13 or 17 to Rozengracht).

◆ *The Theatermuseum is well worth a visit*

TAKING A BREAK

Foodism £ ❶ Easily reached from Dam Square, this small, hip restaurant is awash with bright colours. 🅐 Oude Leliestraat 8 📞 020 427 5103 🆆 www.foodism.nl 🕐 11.30–22.00 Mon–Fri, 11.30–18.00 Sat & Sun

Spanjer & Van Twist £ ❷ One of the best *eetcafés* in the city, for both the atmosphere and the food. 🅐 Leliegracht 60 📞 020 639 0109 🕐 10.00–24.00 🚋 Tram: 13, 14, 17 to Westermarkt

Puccini £–££ ❸ This intimate espresso bar serves delicious breakfasts and lunches. 🅐 Staalstraat 21 📞 020 620 8458 🆆 www.puccini.nl 🕐 08.30–18.00 Mon–Fri, 10.00–18.00 Sat & Sun 🚇 Metro to Waterlooplein

Café Americain ££ ❹ With its ornate stained-glass chandeliers and vast windows, this art nouveau café is a popular meeting point for Amsterdammers. 🅐 Leidsekade 97 📞 020 556 3010 🕐 06.30–23.30 Mon–Fri, 07.00–23.30 Sat & Sun 🚋 Tram: 1, 2 ,5, 6, 10, 17 to Leidseplein

AFTER DARK

RESTAURANTS
De Blauwe Hollander £ ❺ Down-to-earth Dutch restaurant near the Leidseplein with large communal tables. Popular with locals. 🅐 Leidsekruisstraat 28 📞 020 627 0521 🆆 www.deblauwehollander.nl 🕐 12.00–23.00 🚋 Tram: 1, 2, 5, 6, 10, 17 to Leidseplein

Tapas Café Duende £–££ ❻ Smoky, atmospheric tapas restaurant with tapas, sangria and Flamenco at the back. 🅐 Lindengracht 62

☎ 020 420 6692 **🌐** www.cafeduende.nl **🕓** 16.00–01.00 Mon–Thur,
16.00–03.00 Fri & Sat **Ⓝ** Bus: 18, 21, 22 to Prinsengracht

De Belhamel ££ ❼ Overlooking the picturesque Herengracht and
Brouwersgracht canals, this art nouveau restaurant serves seasonal
French–Italian cuisine. A bit pricey but worth it for such splendid
surroundings. **ⓐ** Brouwersgracht 60 **☎** 020 622 1095 **🕓** 18.00–22.00
Sun–Thur, 18.00–22.30 Fri & Sat **Ⓝ** Tram: 1, 2, 5, 13, 17 to Martelaarsgracht

Japanese Pancake World ££ ❽ There's only one cook for this tiny
restaurant so don't expect quick service, but the pancakes are definitely
worth the wait. **ⓐ** Egelantiersdwarsstraat 24A **☎** 020 320 4447
🌐 www.japanesepancakeworld.com **🕓** 12.00–22.00 **Ⓝ** Tram: 6, 13, 14,
17; Bus: 21, 170, 172 to Rozengracht-Westerkerk

Van Puffelen ££ ❾ Canal-side brown café/casual restaurant which
opens up into a floating barge in summer. **ⓐ** Prinsengracht 375–377
☎ 020 624 6270 **🕓** 17.00–24.00 Mon–Wed, 12.00–24.00 Thur–Sun
Ⓝ Tram: 13, 14, or 17 to Westermarkt

Bordewijk £££ ❿ One of Amsterdam's most fashionable eating places,
smart but not stuffy. The menu is French fusion with changing accents
depending on the season. Reservations recommended – book a table
near the window if you can. **ⓐ** Noordermarkt 7 **☎** 020 624 3899
🌐 www.bordewijk.nl **🕓** 18.30–22.30 Tues–Sun **Ⓝ** Tram: 13, 17, 20;
Bus: 21 to Westermarkt

Christophe £££ ⓫ If you want to sample the finest of Amsterdam's
fine dining, look no further. This place has set high standards since it
opened in 1987, and earned its first Michelin star two years later. Dress

is smart casual and the food is French gourmet style with a touch of North Africa reflecting Christophe Royer's Algerian birthplace. ⓐ Leliegracht 46 ⓣ 020 625 0807 ⓦ www.restaurantchristophe.nl ⓛ 18.30–22.30 Tues–Sat ⓝ Tram: 13, 17, 20; Bus: 21 to Westermarkt

BARS & CLUBS

De Admiraal This old tasting house is run by a distillery and is definitely the place to head if you fancy a hard drink and a bit of history. There are usually at least 16 gins and 60 liqueurs on offer. It also serves snacks and proper meals. ⓐ Herengracht 319 ⓣ 020 625 4334 ⓛ 17.00–24.00 Mon–Sat ⓝ Tram: 1, 2, 5 to Spui; Tram: 13 to NZ Voorburgwal

Melkweg The Milky Way is open all day for exhibitions, galleries, food, drink and live music, and all night for DJs and dancing. There is an adjoining café-restaurant and photo gallery. ⓐ Lijnbaansgracht 234A ⓣ 020 531 8181 ⓛ 13.00–05.00 Mon–Fri, 16.00–06.00 Sat & Sun ⓝ Tram: 1, 2, 5, 7, 10 to Leidseplein

Wolvenstraat 23 If you need a bar at breakfast time, the Wolvenstraat is it. That said, its 1970s retro style has made it fashionable at any time of day – hip Amsterdammers like to meet and eat here late at night. ⓐ Wolvenstraat 23 ⓣ 020 320 0843 ⓛ 08.00–01.00 Sun–Thur, 09.00–02.00 Fri & Sat ⓝ Tram: 1, 2, 5 to Spui; Tram: 13 to NZ Voorburgwal

Zebra Lounge Former strip club near the Leidseplein, now one of the trendiest dance clubs in town with a rota of top DJs and guests. Dress smart. ⓐ Korte Leidsedwarsstraat 14 ⓣ 020 612 6153 ⓦ www.the-zebra.nl ⓛ 22.00–02.00 Wed, Thur & Sun, 22.00–03.00 Fri & Sat ⓝ Tram: 1, 2, 5, 6, 10, 17 to Leidseplein

▶ *The miniature city of Madurodam*

Den Haag (The Hague)

Known to the world for being the seat of the International Court of Justice, the principal judicial organ of the UN, The Hague is in fact one of the loveliest cities in the Netherlands. It is worth at least a day trip from Amsterdam, or better still an overnight stay if you can afford the time. It's full of museums, beautiful old buildings and a lively café, bar and restaurant scene. This mix of old and new makes the city both stimulating and relaxing.

The Hague is the country's governmental hub, housing the Dutch Parliament as well as the Permanent Court of Arbitration and The Hague Academy of International Law. Visit if you're interested in history, politics, architecture or the royal family. If you're looking for a day out shopping, bypass The Hague and go straight to Rotterdam (see page 130), which is further south. Only 20 minutes away by train you'll find **Delft**, famous for its charming canals and blue and white pottery.

Tourist information office ⓐ Koningin Julianaplein 30, opposite the Parliament Buildings ⓣ 070 363 5676 ⓦ www.denhaag.com Ⓝ Tram: 1, 16, 17; Bus: 4, 5, 22

GETTING THERE

The Hague is 56 km (35 miles) southwest of Amsterdam. It is two hours away by train and a return ticket costs €17.40. Driving, depending on traffic conditions, is usually slightly faster. There is no metro in The Hague so most people get around by tram or bus, which operate from directly outside the train station. A *strippenkart* covers six journeys and costs €6.50.

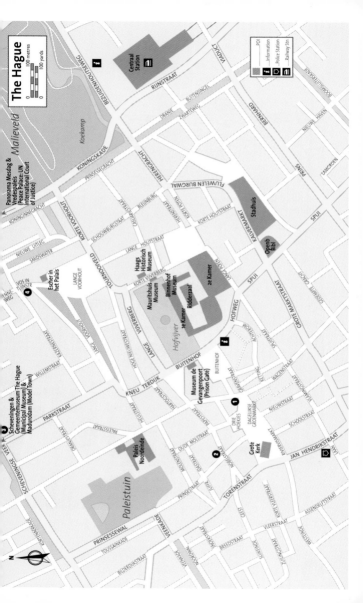

The Hague

0 — 100 metres
0 — 100 yards

POI
i Information
Police Station
Railway Stn

Malieveld

Beatrixlaan

Bezuidenhoutseweg

Centraal Station

Rijnstraat

Buitensingel

Oranje Buitenweg

Nieuwe Haven

Bernhard

Prins

Koetkamp

Koningskade

Prinsessegracht

Herengracht

Fluwelen Burgwal

Bleijenburg

Kort Voorhout

Casuariestraat

Korte Voorhout

Spui

Spui

Grote Marktstraat

Panorama Mesdag & Vredespaleis (Peace Palace) UN International Court of Justice

Koningin Sophiestraat

Nieuwe Uitleg

Smidswater

Lange Voorhout

Tournooiveld

Lange Vijverberg

Kort Vijverberg

Kazernestraat

Kneuterdijk

Hofweg

Rijswijkstraat

Kalvermarkt

Openb Bibl

Stadhuis

Escher in het Palais

Vos in Tuinstr

Panne Weg

Scheveningse Veer

Scheveningen & Gemeentemuseum The Hague (Municipal Museum) & Madurodam (Model Town)

Parkstraat

Mallestraat

Oranjestraat

Willemstraat

Nieuwe Schoolstraat

Lange Houtstraat

Haags Historisch Museum

Mauritshuis Museum

Lange Vijverberg

Hoge Nieuwstraat

Korte Vijverberg

Hofvijver

Binnenhof Museum

Buitenhof

Buitenhof

Plein

1e Kamer   Ridderzaal

2e Kamer

Museum de Gevangenpoort (Prison Gate)

Paleis Noordeinde

Paleistuin

Prinsessewal

Toussainkade

Bilderdijkstraat

Prinsessegracht

Veenkade

Prinsegracht

Oude Molstraat

Noordeinde

Hoogstraat

Drie Hoekjes

Dagelijkse Groenmarkt

Grote Kerk

Prinsestraat

Molenstraat

Juffrouw Idastraat

Achterom

Kettingstraat

Wagenstraat

Nieuwstraat

Venestraat

Torenstraat

Assendelftstraat

Geest

Vleerstraat

Breedstraat

Jan Hendrikstraat

Schoolstraat

Zuidwal

N

● *The Binnenhof in The Hague*

CAPITAL IDEA

Although the Dutch Parliament is in The Hague, leading many people to assume it is the capital, that honour belongs to Amsterdam. The Hague is the capital of the Netherlands' South Holland province.

SIGHTS & ATTRACTIONS

Dutch Parliament Buildings

The 13th-century *Ridderzaal* (Knights' Hall) stands at the centre of the *Binnenhof*, the old Dutch Parliament's Inner Court. Parliament today meets in modern buildings on the south side of the complex, but the Queen still delivers an annual speech from her throne in the *Ridderzaal*. The only way to look around is on one of the regular guided tours, which take 30–45 mins. ⓐ Binnenhof ❶ 070 364 6144 ❶ 070 364 5544 ⓦ www.binnenhof.nl ❶ Tours 10.00–15.45 Mon–Sat ⓝ Tram: 1, 16, 17; Bus: 4, 5, 22. Admission charge

Madurodam (Model Town)

A paradoxical place – a vast miniature city encompassing the edited highlights of the Netherlands. From Schiphol Airport to the bulb fields, Delft to Utrecht and The Hague's Peace Palace to Amsterdam's Royal Palace, it's all here compressed on a 1:25 scale. Great place to take the kids. ⓐ George Maduroplein 1 ❶ 070 416 2400 ❶ 070 351 2185 ⓦ www.madurodam.nl ⓔ info@madurodam.nl ❶ 09.00–20.00 Apr–June; 09.00–22.00 July & Aug; 09.00–18.00 Sept–Mar ⓝ Tram: 9; Bus: 22. Admission charge

THE HEDGE

The Hague's unusual name *Den Haag* (The Hedge) dates back almost 800 years. The *Ridderzaal* castle that was built here in the 13th century was once the home of the Counts of Holland. Prior to its construction, the Counts had a hunting lodge on the same site, which was surrounded by a hedge. The city that grew up around the castle was called 's *Gravenhage* (the Count's Hedge). Over time, this was simplified to *Den Haag*.

Museum de Gevangenpoort (Prison Gate)

The collection of torture instruments and the torture room always get people's attention here, but there's a lot more to see in this 15th-century former prison. There are guided tours on the hour every hour but ring ahead to check which language the tour is going to be in. There are extra English-language tours in summer. ⓐ Buitenhof 33 ❶ 070 346 0861 ❶ 070 361 4262 ⓦ www.gevangenpoort.nl ⓔ info@gevangenpoort.nl ⓛ 11.00–17.00 Tues–Fri, 12.00–17.00 Sat & Sun, last tour 16.00 ⓝ Tram: 1, 16, 17; Bus: 4, 5, 22. Admission charge

Scheveningen

It only takes about 15 minutes on a tram to get to this beach resort, which is practically a suburb of The Hague. Take the chance to relax by walking along the beach, admiring the pier and the grand old seafront buildings or visiting the aquarium. ⓝ Tram: 1

Vredespaleis (UN International Court of Justice)

The seat of the International Court of Justice is here, also known as the Peace Palace. It's an impressive building, founded in 1899

◆ *The Hague is a lively mix of old and new*

and paid for by the American philanthropist Andrew Carnegie.
There are guided tours of the buildings when the courts are
not in session, so check and book a tour in advance if you want
to visit. ❷ Carnegieplein 2 ❶ 070 302 4242 ❶ 070 302 4132
Ⓦ www.vredespaleis.nl ❷ guidedtours@planet.nl ❶ Tours at
10.00, 11.00, 14.00, 15.00 & 16.00 Mon–Fri ❷ Tram: 1; Bus: 4, 13.
Admission charge

CULTURE

Escher in het Palais (Escher in the Palace)

The Lange Voorhout Palace in the old city centre was once a
royal palace. Inside it these days you'll find the world's biggest
collection of work by the Dutch graphic artist Maurits Cornelis
Escher. Almost everything he ever produced is housed here,
including his famous 'impossible' works such as *Waterfall*, where
water appears to flow uphill. The café, set in the former Queen's
kitchen, is also good. ❷ Lange Voorhout 74 ❶ 070 427 7730 ❶ 070
427 7731 Ⓦ www.escherinhetpaleis.nl ❷ info@escherinhetpaleis.nl
❶ 11.00–17.00 Tues–Sun ❷ Tram: 16, 17; Bus: 4, 5, 22. Admission charge

Gemeentemuseum (Municipal Museum)

The city's main art and crafts museum, with works by Picasso,
Kandinsky and leading 20th-century Dutch artist Piet Mondriaan.
There's some Delft pottery and local silver, for which The Hague
is well known. You'll also find collections of musical instruments,
fashion and photography, with changing temporary exhibitions.
❷ Stadhouderslaan 41 ❶ 070 338 1111 ❶ 070 338 1112
Ⓦ www.gemeentemuseum.nl ❷ info@gemeentemuseum.nl
❶ 11.00–17.00 Tues–Sun ❷ Tram: 17; Bus: 4, 14. Admission charge

Haags Historisch Museum (Historical Museum)

The highlight of this well-presented historical museum is its series of temporary exhibitions, exploring colourful and unexpected aspects of Dutch history such as the growth of Indonesian rock music or aboriginal art. The semi-permanent collection, covering the 1600s to the present day, is dry but informative. ⓐ Korte Vijverberg 7 ⓣ 070 364 6940 ⓕ 070 364 6942 ⓦ www.haagshistorischmuseum.nl ⓔ info@haagshistorischmuseum.nl ⓛ 10.00–17.00 Tues–Fri, 12.00–17.00 Sat & Sun ⓝ Tram: 1, 16, 17; Bus: 4, 5, 22. Admission charge

Mauritshuis Museum

Works by artists from Rembrandt to Andy Warhol are on display in this stunning neoclassical building next to the Binnenhof, including Warhol's portrait of Queen Beatrix. Vermeer's *View of Delft* and *Girl with a Pearl Earring* offer a bit of a contrast and there are also paintings here by Rubens, Van Hals, Jan Steen and Van Dijck. ⓐ Korte Vijverberg 8 ⓣ 070 302 3435 ⓕ 070 365 3819 ⓦ www.mauritshuis.nl ⓔ communicatie@mauritshuis.nl ⓛ 10.00–17.00 Mon–Sat, 11.00–17.00 Sun & holidays, April–Sept; 10.00–17.00 Tues–Sat, 11.00–17.00 Sun & holidays, Oct–Mar ⓝ Tram: 1. Admission charge

Panorama Mesdag

This unusual attraction has to be seen to be believed. It's a 360 degree cylindrical painting of the sand dunes at the nearby seaside resort of Scheveningen (see page 124), which you can stand inside. It's about 14 m (46 ft) high and was produced by the noted 19th-century local artist Hendrik Willem Mesdag. ⓐ Zeestraat 65 ⓣ 070 364 4544 ⓕ 070 345 0431 ⓦ www.panorama-mesdag.com ⓔ info@panorama-mesdeg.com ⓛ 10.00–17.00 Mon–Sat, 12.00–17.00 Sun & holidays ⓝ Tram: 1; Bus: 4, 5, 22. Admission charge

TAKING A BREAK & AFTER DARK

RESTAURANTS
't Goude Hooft ££ ❶ Inn dating to 1492 (though its current home was built in the 1930s) with a fabulous central location. Classic Dutch dishes include potato croquettes, pea soup with sausages and apple tart. ⓐ Dagelijkse Groenmarkt 13 ❶ 070 346 9713 Ⓦ www.tgoudehooft.nl ❷ 8.00–late

Puck Food and Wines ££ ❷ Named after the owner's daughter, Puck combines French cooking with Californian wine. Classy yet affordable and friendly. ⓐ Prinsestraat 33 ❶ 070 427 7649 ❷ 18.00–late Tues–Sat

Ramakien ££ ❸ The place for authentic Thai cuisine, with the dishes cooked lightly but full of flavour and spice. Excellent fish. ⓐ Laan van Meerdervoort 542C ❶ 070 356 2352 ❷ 17.00–23.00 Wed–Mon ❷ Tram: 3 to Goudenregenstraat

Restaurant Julien £££ ❹ One of the top spots in town, with a fabulously grand interior and the best contemporary Dutch cooking. Keep it for a treat or splurge for lunch if on a day trip from Amsterdam. ⓐ Vos in Tuinstraat 2a ❶ 070 365 8602 Ⓦ www.julien.nl ❷ 12.00–14.00 & 17.30–22.00 ❷ Tram: 9 to Malieveld; Tram: 16, 17 to Korte Voorhout

BARS & CLUBS
De Paap Not to be confused with De Paas, De Paap is a café bar with live gigs by emerging new bands. The whole of this street is a trendy place to go at night. ⓐ Papestraat 32 ❶ 070 365 2002 ❷ 19.00–04.00 Tues–Fri & Sun, 17.00–04.00 Sat ❷ Tram: 2, 3, 6 to Grote Markt

De Paas Like Amsterdam, The Hague has its brown cafés and this is one of the best. It's certainly got one of the best selections of beer, with over 150 different brands to choose from. ⓐ Dunne Bierkade 16A ⓣ 070 360 0019 ⓦ www.depaas.nl ⓛ 15.00–01.00 Sun–Thur, 15.00–01.30 Fri & Sat

Paard van Troje (Trojan Horse) Offering everything from funk, dance hall and jazz to ska music and stand-up comedy, this venue can house up to 1,100 party people and has showcased top acts such as Kane and DJs Deep Dish. The place to try out your dancing shoes. ⓐ Prinsengracht 12 ⓣ 070 360 1838 ⓦ www.paard.nl ⓔ info@paard.nl ⓛ Times vary

ACCOMMODATION

For further advice on accommodation in The Hague and for reservations, contact the tourist office accommodation department on ⓣ 070 338 5815 ⓕ 070 346 2412 ⓦ www.denhaag.com ⓔ reserveringen@spdh.net

Hotel Mimosa £ Inexpensive family hotel right by the sea in Scheveningen. Perfect for a cheap, quick break and a breath of fresh seaside air. ⓐ Renbaanstraat 18–24 ⓣ 070 354 8137 ⓦ www.hotelmimosa.nl ⓝ Tram: 1, 9; Bus: 22

Le Méridien Hotel des Indes ££ One of the best-value 5-star hotels in town. Visiting VIPs stay here all the time. ⓐ Lange Voorhout 54–56 ⓣ 070 361 2345 ⓦ www.hague.lemeridien.com ⓝ Tram: 9 plus a short walk

Rotterdam

Rotterdam is the Netherlands' second biggest city and is very different from the capital. In some ways it's less exciting, but in others it's fresher and funkier. It also seems much bigger, because the centre sprawls whereas Amsterdam is kept compact by its canals.

Rotterdam is the place to go for stunning modern architecture, museums and shopping. Its port, one of the biggest and busiest in the world, is also an incredible sight. Considered Amsterdam's younger, more commercial sister, the city boasts an international population and follows a faster rhythm. One drawback – most people who work here live in the suburbs, making the city surprisingly quiet at night.

Tourist information office ⓐ Coolsingel 5 ⓣ 0900 403 4065
ⓕ 010 271 0128 ⓦ www.rotterdam.info ⓔ info@rotterdam-store.nl
ⓛ 09.00–17.30 Mon–Thur, 09.00–21.00 Fri, 09.00–17.00 Sat,
10.00–17.00 Sun ⓝ Metro to Stadhuis

GETTING THERE

Rotterdam boasts a wide network of motorways and roads and an extensive public transportation system. Rotterdam Centraal Station is a major hub in the Dutch railway network and there are six direct connections to Amsterdam every hour. Travel time is one hour and a ticket costs around €23. Rotterdam is also just 15 minutes from The Hague by train.

Eurolines coaches stop directly in front of Centraal Station and if you opt to drive from Amsterdam, take the A4 then the A13. Traffic tends to be heavy both in and surrounding the city.

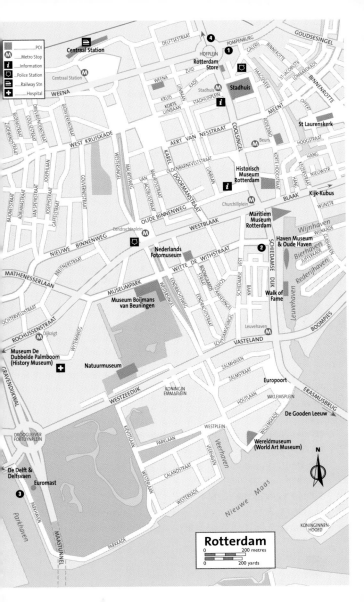

Rotterdam

Legend:
- POI
- Ⓜ Metro Stop
- ℹ Information
- Police Station
- Railway Stn
- ✚ Hospital

Centraal Station

GOUDSESINGEL
DELFTSESTRAAT
POMPENBURG
HOFPLEIN ❶
Rotterdam Store
BINNENROTTE
GALERI
HALSEKADE
ST LAURENSKADE
LOMBARDKADE
BINNENROTTE
Centraal Station Ⓜ
WEENA
ZUID
KADE
Stadhuis ℹ **Stadhuis**
MEENT
KRUIS
LIJNBAAN
STADHUISPLEIN
WEENA
KORTE LIJNBAAN
AERT VAN NESSTRAAT
COOLSINGEL
St Laurenskerk
HOOGSTRAAT
WEST KRUISKADE
KAREL DOORMANSTRAAT
OUDENBARNEVELTSTRAAT
VAN JACOBSTRAAT
MAURITSWEG
WESTEINDE
COLVINISTRAAT
JOSEPHLAAN
JOSEPHSTRAAT
BAJONETSTRAAT
ADRIANASTRAAT
VAN SPEYKSTRAAT
GAFFELSTRAAT
Ⓜ Beurs
KORTE HOOGSTRAAT
HANG
NIEUWSTR
BLAAK
Kijk-Kubus
WIJNSTR
Historisch Museum Rotterdam ℹ
LIJNBAAN
OUDE BINNENWEG
NIEUWE BINNENWEG
Eendrachtsplein Ⓜ
Eendrachtsplein
WESTBLAAK
Churchillplein Ⓜ
Maritiem Museum Rotterdam
Haven Museum & Oude Haven
Wijnhaven
WINKADE
Bierhaven
Rederijhaven
Leuvehaven
❷
NETTENKADE
Nederlands Fotomuseum
WITTE DE WITHSTRAAT
SCHIEDAMSE DIJK
Walk of Fame
MATHENESSERLAAN
WESTERSINGEL
BOOMPJESHOF
EENDRACHTSWEG
BOOMGAARDSTRAAT
SCHIEDAMSESINGEL
SCHIEDAMSESINGEL
BAAN
WEST ZEEDIJK
MUSEUMPARK
Museum Boijmans van Beuningen
Ⓜ Leuvehaven
VASTELAND
ROCHUSSENSTRAAT
Dijkzigt Ⓜ
WYTEMAWEG
✚ **Museum De Dubbelde Palmboom (History Museum)**
Natuurmuseum
ZALMHAVEN
ZALMSTRAAT
Europoort
KONINGIN EMMAPLEIN
GRAVENDIJKWAL
HOUTLAAN
WILLEMSPLEIN
ERASMUSBRUG
DROOGLEEVER FORTUYNPLEIN
WESTZEEDIJK
PARKLAAN
WESTPLEIN
WILLEMSKADE
De Gooden Leeuw ⛵
KIEVITSLAAN
WILLEMSKADE
VEERHAVEN
Wereldmuseum (World Art Museum)
WESTERLAAN
CALANDSTRAAT
VEERKADE
N
De Delft & Delfsvaen
Euromast
❸
Parkhaven
PARKKADE
WESTERKADE
Nieuwe Maas
MAASTUNNEL
PARKHAVEN
KONINGINNEN-HOOFD

Rotterdam
| 0 | 200 metres |
| 0 | 200 yards |

OUT OF TOWN

Trams, buses and the metro connect with each other throughout the city centre and you can use the ferry or water taxi when crossing the broad, rolling Mass River.

SIGHTS & ATTRACTIONS

De Delft and Delfsvaen

Go back in time and watch a fantastic 18th-century ship being reconstructed in a shipyard. The Delft was shipwrecked and on board this ongoing reconstruction you can see not only the treasures that were recovered but also the craftsmen at work on their various specialist tasks. There are great waterfront views, too, and a chance to see the area known as Delfshaven. This was originally the port for Delft and has survived as a wonderful old quarter of Rotterdam, with a definite maritime atmosphere and plenty of cafés and bars. ⓐ Schiehaven 15 ⓣ 010 276 0115 ⓕ 010 244 0362 ⓦ www.dedelft.nl ⓔ info@dedelft.nl ⓛ 10.00–16.00 Tues–Fri, 10.00–17.00 Sat & Sun ⓝ Tram: 8

Euromast

If you've no head for heights, this sight is not for you. The Euromast first takes you to a height of 100 m (328 ft), where there's a breathtaking view of Rotterdam and its vast harbours. For the brave, you can then take a ride to the very top on the Euroscoop, 185 m (607 ft) in the air. ⓐ Parkhaven 20 ⓣ 010 436 4811 ⓦ www.euromast.nl ⓔ info@euromast.nl ⓛ 09.30–23.00 Apr–Sept; 10.00–23.00 Oct–Mar ⓝ Tram: 8; Metro to Dijkzicht. Admission charge

Guided tours of the ports

The best way to see both the vast ports of Rotterdam, which are truly incredible, is on the Spido boat. The harbour tour lasts about

75 minutes and an introductory DVD sets the scene. As well as seeing the harbour you get excellent views of some of the city's quirky architecture. Tours and day trips during July and August range from 75 minutes to seven hours. ⊙ Willemsplein 85 (at the base of the Erasmus Bridge) ☎ 010 275 9988 🖷 010 412 4788 Ⓦ www.spido.nl Ⓔ spido@spido.nl Ⓝ Tram: 7 to Willemsplein; Metro to Leuvehaven

Haven Museum and Oude Haven

The older parts of Rotterdam's extensive harbours are here at Oude Haven, along with a great indoor/outdoor working museum that really gives you a feel for life in the shipyards over the years. Old boats are restored here and you can also take a steamboat ride out into the harbour. ⊙ Leuvehaven 50–72 ☎ 010 404 8072 🖷 010 404 9508 Ⓦ www.havenmuseum.nl Ⓔ info@havenmuseum.nl 🕓 10.00–17.00 Tues–Fri, 11.00–17.00 Sat & Sun Ⓝ Tram: 1, 8, 20; Bus: 32, 49; Metro to Beurs or Churchillplein

Historisch Museum (Historical Museum)

Housed in the only remaining 17th-century building in Rotterdam, this museum tells the story of the city's history using everything from domestic artefacts to grand documents. There's an extensive print and sketch collection. ⊙ Korte Hoogstraat 31 ☎ 010 217 6767 Ⓦ www.hmr.rotterdam.nl Ⓔ info@hmr.rotterdam.nl 🕓 10.00–17.00 Tues–Sun Ⓝ Tram: 1, 8, 20, 23; Metro to Beurs. Admission charge

Maritiem Museum (Maritime Museum)

This recently renovated museum really does Rotterdam's impressive maritime history justice. The interactive exhibits, including a 15 m (49 ft) model of the modern port, are impressive and there are lots of

ARCHITECTURE

Rotterdam has become renowned for its startling modern architecture, which manages to combine the Dutch flair for quirky originality with stylish modern concepts. Simply walking around the city is an experience, as you never know what you are going to see. The simple Euromast thrusts into the air like an Olympic torch and down at the harbour you can see a building that seems to lean over at an alarming angle. It's the KPN Telecom building, designed by Renzo Piano, the man who came up with the inside-out Pompidou Centre in Paris.

The best-loved examples of Rotterdam's architecture are probably the fun-looking **Kijk-Kubus** (Cube Houses ⓐ Overblaak 70 ⓣ 010 414 2285 ⓦ www.kubuswoning.nl ⓛ 11.00–17.00 ⓜ Metro: Rotterdam Blaak; Tram: 21). It is hard to see how people can actually live in these angled cubes supported by a few poles. Fortunately, one is open for visitors.

To see this and other examples of Rotterdam's unique buildings, it's worth taking an organised Architecture Tour, which you can book through the tourist office or a travel agent.

activities for children. ⓐ Leuvehaven 1 ⓣ 010 413 2680 ⓕ 010 413 7342 ⓦ www.maritiemmuseum.nl ⓔ info@maritiemmuseum.nl ⓛ 10.00–17.00 Tues–Sat, 11.00–17.00 Sun & holidays; also open 10.00–17.00 Mon, July–Aug & school holidays ⓜ Tram: 1, 8, 20; Bus: 32, 49; Metro to Beurs or Churchillplein. Admission charge

◀ *Rotterdam's wacky Cube Houses*

Museum De Dubbelde Palmboom (History Museum)

This 19th-century warehouse in the old port at Delfshaven houses a museum focusing on Rotterdam's history as a port and on the human side of the city's past. The personal stories are truly compelling. ⓐ Voorhaven 12 ⓣ 010 476 1533 ⓦ www.dedubbeldepalmboom.nl ⓔ info@hmr.rotterdam.nl ⓛ 10.00–17.00 Tues–Sun ⓝ Tram: 4, 8; Metro to Delfshaven. Admission charge

Natuurmuseum (Natural History Museum)

This villa houses an old-fashioned natural history museum, displaying mostly stuffed animals and birds, some beautiful butterflies and some scary bugs. The highlight is the 15 m (49 ft) skeleton of a sperm whale. ⓐ Westzeedijk 345, Museumpark ⓣ 010 436 4222 ⓦ www.nmr.nl ⓔ natuurmuseum@nmr.nl ⓛ 10.00–17.00 Tues–Sat, 11.00–17.00 Sun ⓝ Tram: 5, 8. Admission charge

CULTURE

Museum Boijmans van Beuningen (Boijmans Museum)

The city's main art museum has a fine collection, ranging from the Old Masters to modern works by artists such as Kandinsky, Dalì and Magritte. There are also pieces by Van Gogh, Gaugin, Monet, Dégas, Titian, Rembrandt, Breughel and Hieronymous Bosch. ⓐ Museumpark 18–20 ⓣ 010 441 9400 ⓕ 010 436 0500 ⓦ www.boijmans.rotterdam.nl ⓔ info@boijmans.rotterdam.nl ⓛ 11.00–17.00 Tues–Sun ⓝ Tram: 5. Admission charge

Nederlands Fotomuseum

The Dutch don't have a reputation for photography, but this national museum suggests that they could. It has an archive of about four million negatives from more than 80 of the country's leading photographers, displayed on a rotating basis. There are also temporary photography exhibitions. ⓐ Witte de Withstraat 63 ☎ 010 203 0405 ⓦ www.nederlandsfotomuseum.nl ⓔ info@nederlandsfotomuseum.nl ⏰ 10.00–17.00 Tues–Sun ⓝ Tram: 5, 8

Wereldmuseum (World Art Museum)

The roots of this fascinating museum hail from the spice trade, when Dutch sailors brought back interesting objects from Indonesia. There is now a collection of more than 200,000 items celebrating the arts and crafts of cultures all over the world. There are especially good displays on Islamic and Aboriginal arts and the 19th-century photographic archive is impressive. ⓐ Willemskade 25 ☎ 010 270 7172 ⓦ www.wereldmuseum.rotterdam.nl ⓔ bibliotheek@wereldmuseum.rotterdam.nl ⏰ 10.00–17.00 Tues–Sun ⓝ Tram: 7. Admission charge

RETAIL THERAPY

Rotterdam is a great place for fashion enthusiasts. You'll find stylish boutiques, stores, cafés and gift-shops in the area between Kruiskade and Van Oldenbarneveltstraat, close to Centraal Station. If you're looking for top-brand men's and women's footware, try **Shoebaloo** (ⓐ Kruiskade 57C ⓦ www.shoebaloo.nl ⏰ 12.00–18.00 Mon, 10.00–18.00 Tues–Thurs & Sat, 10.00–21.00 Fri, 13.00–18.00 Sun). Another great area for shopaholics is Hillegersberg, just north of the city centre.

Rotterdam has the largest market square in the Netherlands, the **Binnenrotte** (⏰ 09.00–17.00 Tues & Sat, Jan–Apr; 09.00–17.00 Tues, Sat & Sun, May–Dec), which is filled with around 500 stalls selling all sorts of food and drink, plants, fresh flowers and second-hand goods.

● *Rotterdam is brilliant for shopping*

Rotterdam is such a hotspot for shoppers that the tourist board even puts out a special booklet with eight shopping routes you can do on foot. These include the historic part of the city, near the waterfront, the hip and freaky and the chic. It's worth picking one up.

TAKING A BREAK & AFTER DARK

RESTAURANTS

Thai Thani £ ❶ This Thai place serves the real thing – a subtly flavoured menu comprising all the traditional favourites and a few surprises. The squid in yellow curry sauce is fantastic. ⓐ Pompenburg 652 ⓣ 010 413 3896 ⓛ 17.00–22.30 ⓝ Bus: 38, 45, 49; Tram: 3, 4, 5, 6, 7, 9, 13, 20 to Hofplein; Metro to Stadhuis

Met de Franse Slag ££ ❷ A place to try some good Belgian cuisine. There's an intimate atmosphere here and a decent wine list, making for a very relaxed evening. ❸ Schilderstraat 20–22A ❶ 010 413 0143 ⓦ www.metdefranseslag.nl ⓛ 17.00–late Ⓜ Metro to Churchillplein

Pancake Boat ££ ❸ What could be more Dutch than eating pancakes on a boat? Once the ship sets sail you can eat your fill of all kinds of flavours available at the buffet. But remember, you've only got an hour. ❸ Parkhaven, opposite the Euromast ❶ 010 436 7295 ⓦ www.pannenkoekenboot.nl ⓛ 16.30, 17.30, 18.00 & 19.00 Fri–Sun & Wed Ⓝ Tram: 8 to Euromast

St Paul's £££ ❹ This is allegedly a French restaurant, but its menu is truly international. There are some quirky combinations, such as chicken stuffed with crab and served with a Yorkshire pudding – but it usually works. Sit back and enjoy it. ❸ Kleiweg 89 ❶ 010 418 5274 ⓛ 18.00–22.00 Wed–Sun Ⓝ Bus: 35, 49; Tram: 4

BARS & CLUBS

Baja Beach Club Miles from any beach, slap in the middle of the city centre, this club does aim for a beach party feel. Girls get free champagne all night on Thursdays. ❸ Karel Doormanstraat 10–12 ❶ 010 213 1180 ⓦ www.baja.nl ⓛ 22.30–05.00 Thur–Sun Ⓜ Metro to Eendrachtsplein

Coconuts A Caribbean-style dance bar/restaurant with a friendly, festive atmosphere. Good cocktail menu and music from DJs. ❸ Stadhuisplien 19 ❶ 010 413 0804 ⓦ www.coconuts.nl Ⓜ Metro to Stadhuisplein

De Gooden Leeuw Well-established English-style pub with a pool table and basic pub food. ❸ Ijsselmondsehoofd 1–3 ❶ 010 482 7569

🕐 07.00–24.00 Mon–Thur, 07.00–02.00 Fri, 13.00–02.00 Sat,
14.00–19.00 Sun Ⓝ Bus: 75 to Ijsselmondsehoofd

Paddy Murphy's Not very traditionally Dutch, but with live music
every night of the week, usually until late, this is where lots of
Rotterdammers hang out. Great buzz. ⓐ Rodezand 15 ☎ 010 411 0078
Ⓦ www.paddymurphys.nl Ⓝ Metro to Beurs

ACCOMMODATION

HOTELS
Maritime Hotel Rotterdam £ Excellent location near the waterfront
if you want to explore the maritime side of the city. A 3-star hotel
with 165 rooms and cheap rates, sometimes offering special deals.
ⓐ Willemskade 13 ☎ 010 201 0900 Ⓦ www.maritimehotel.nl
ⓔ info@maritimehotel.nl Ⓝ Tram: 7; Metro to Leuvehaven

Hotel New York ££ If you can afford to splash out a bit, this 19th-century
head office of the Holland–America Line has been transformed into
a modern 4-star hotel. ⓐ Koninginnenhoofd 1 ☎ 010 439 0500
☎ 010 484 2701 Ⓦ www.hotelnewyork.nl Ⓝ Metro to Wilhelminaplein;
Tram: 20

HOSTELS
Stayokay Rotterdam £ Rotterdam's city hostel is very central,
very comfortable and has 100 beds available in single, double and
quadruple rooms. ⓐ Rochussenstraat 107–109 ☎ 010 436 5763
Ⓦ www.stayokay.com ⓔ rotterdam@stayokay.nl

▶ *Amsterdam's excellent tram network makes travelling around the city a pleasure*

Directory

GETTING THERE

By air

Amsterdam's Schiphol Airport is about 18 km (11 miles) southwest of the city centre and is well served by scheduled flights from all over Europe and beyond. The flight time from London is about 45 minutes.

bmi fly from London Heathrow ☎ 0870 607 0555 ⓦ www.flybmi.com

bmibaby fly from Nottingham and Birmingham ☎ 0870 264 2229 ⓦ www.bmibaby.com

British Airways fly from London Heathrow, Gatwick and Manchester ☎ 0870 850 9850 ⓦ www.britishairways.com

easyjet fly from Belfast, Bristol, Edinburgh, Liverpool and London's Stansted, Luton and Gatwick airports ☎ 0871 244 2366 ⓦ www.easyjet.com

Jet2 fly from Leeds-Bradford ☎ 0870 737 8282 ⓦ www.jet2.com

KLM fly from London Heathrow, London City and numerous UK regional airports ☎ 0870 243 0541 ⓦ www.klm.com

Scotairways fly from Southampton ☎ 0870 606 0707 ⓦ www.scotairways.co.uk

Many people are aware that air travel emits CO_2 which contributes to climate change. You may be interested in the possibility of lessening the environmental impact of your flight through the charity Climate Care, which offsets your CO_2 by funding environmental projects around the world. Visit ⓦ www.climatecare.org

By road

There are ferry services (see page 144) if you wish to take your car to Amsterdam, and a network of good fast roads from elsewhere in

Europe. But Amsterdam's not the best city to explore by car – if it's not essential for your trip, leave it at home.

By rail

Dutchflyer offer good value all-inclusive rail and sail tickets from the UK to Amsterdam. Ⓦ www.dutchflyer.co.uk.

Eurostar services to Brussels allow an onward connection direct to Amsterdam, with a total journey time of 5–6 hours from the UK. ⓣ 0870 518 6186 Ⓦ www.eurostar.com

There are good rail connections between Amsterdam and many major continental European cities. See **Rail Europe** ⓣ 0870 584 8848 Ⓦ www.raileurope.co.uk

⬥ *Planes lined up at Schiphol Airport*

🔺 *Amsterdam Centraal*

The **Thomas Cook European Rail Timetable** has up-to-date schedules for all services. ☎ 01733 416477 (UK) or 1 800 322 3834 (USA)
ⓦ www.thomascookpublishing.com

By water
To reach Amsterdam by ferry from the UK involves going either to Rotterdam or to the Hook of Holland, then driving or taking an onward rail connection to Amsterdam.
P&O Ferries have daily services from Hull to Rotterdam.
☎ 0870 520 2020 ⓦ www.poferries.com
Stena Line sails twice daily from Harwich to the Hook of Holland.
☎ 0870 570 7070 ⓦ www.stenaline.com

ENTRY FORMALITIES

Citizens of the UK, Republic of Ireland and other EU countries, the USA, Canada, Australia and New Zealand do not require a visa for stays of up to 90 days in the Netherlands. Citizens from other countries, as well as those wishing to stay longer than 90 days, will require a visa. A valid passport is always necessary.

Visitors to the Netherlands from within the EU are entitled to bring their personal effects and goods for personal consumption, including a maximum of 800 cigarettes and 10 litres of spirits. Those entering from outside the EU may bring in 200 cigarettes (or 250 grams tobacco or 50 cigars) and two litres of non-sparkling wine plus one litre of strong spirit or two litres of sparkling wine or fortified wine.

MONEY

The Dutch currency is the euro (€), divided into 100 cents. Notes are in denominations of 5, 10, 20, 50, 100, 200 and 500 euros; coins in 1 or 2 euros and 1, 2, 5, 10, 20 and 50 cents.

There are numerous banks, ATMs and bureaux de change in central Amsterdam, as well as in Rotterdam and The Hague. While

TRAVEL INSURANCE

It is strongly recommended that you take out adequate personal travel insurance for the trip, covering medical expenses, loss, theft, repatriation, personal liability and cancellation expenses. If you are travelling in your own vehicle you should also check that you are appropriately insured and have all the relevant documents and your driving licence with you.

credit cards are widely accepted, many smaller establishments will insist on cash.

HEALTH, SAFETY & CRIME

Tap water in Amsterdam is perfectly safe to drink unless marked otherwise and food hygiene generally is to a high standard. The Dutch healthcare system is first class and EU citizens are entitled to free or reduced-price health care on production of a valid European Health Insurance Card (EHIC). See Ⓦ www.dh.gov.uk/travellers for more information.

Crime is not a big issue in Amsterdam, although there is a drug problem. Be careful around Centraal Station and the red light district, especially late at night. Also watch out for pickpockets and fraudsters. **Police stations** are located at ⓐ Beursstraat 33, Nieuwezijds Voorburgwal 104, Keizerstraat 3 ⓣ 0900 8844. You can report

lost property, theft, assault and hate/discrimination crimes.

Lost Property ❷ Stephensonstraat 18, near Amstel station
📞 020 559 3005

OPENING HOURS

Shop opening hours vary. Many are open longer on Thursdays, then open later the next morning. It's also fairly common for stores in the city centre to open on a Sunday afternoon and get off to a leisurely start on Monday mornings.

Museums are typically open 10.00–17.00, but close on Sunday mornings. Some smaller attractions also close on Mondays.

Banks normally open 09.00–16.00 Mon–Fri. Some open longer on Thursday, while others open on Saturday morning instead.

🔻 *The Scheepvaart Museum in Amsterdam*

TOILETS

Public toilets are not widespread in Amsterdam. The ones that do exist are usually very clean, but they do carry a small charge. For men there are a limited number of French-style toilets around the streets. The main option is to use a bar, café or hotel, though in the first two it is considered polite to buy something.

CHILDREN

Amsterdam is usually thought of as a city for singles, party groups and couples on romantic breaks, but there's plenty for families to do too. Children are welcomed almost everywhere, although you may want to keep them out of the red light district.

In terms of museums and attractions, the interactive science and technology centre NEMO (see page 65) is aimed directly at educating and entertaining the kids. The Tropenmuseum Junior (see page 86), is a section of the Tropenmuseum that teaches children about the cultures of the world.

If you're in Amsterdam for the weekend, plan ahead and book your child into the Kinderkookkafe (● Vondelpark 6b (Overtoom 325) ● 020 625 3257 ● www.kinderkookkafe.nl ● Tram: 1, 17 to JP Heyestraat), where they can spend Saturday or Sunday afternoon learning to cook and serve you the finished meal at the end. Or visit the Vondelpark (see page 95), where there are plenty of playgrounds and other activities.

If visiting Rotterdam don't miss the Maritime Museum (see page 133), which explores Dutch sea heritage in a way that deliberately provides lots of hands-on activities for children.

● *Kids will enjoy the Maritime Museum in Rotterdam*

COMMUNICATIONS

Internet

There are several internet cafés in the city centre.

Easyinternetcafé ⓐ Damrak 33 ⓛ 09.00–22.00

Internet City ⓐ Nieuwendijk 76 ⓛ 10.00–24.00

Phone

Most public phone boxes take either credit cards or phonecards. You can buy phonecards in post offices, tourist information centres and tobacconists.

The Netherlands has warmly embraced the mobile phone revolution and a large number of service providers in the UK and other countries have a network available in Amsterdam. You can also buy a SIM card for use in the Netherlands to replace your own while you are away.

TELEPHONING THE NETHERLANDS

To call Amsterdam from overseas, dial the international access code from your country (00 from the UK), then the code for the Netherlands (31), then the area code without the first zero (eg 20 for Amsterdam or 70 for The Hague). Then dial the number you require, which will usually be another seven digits.

TELEPHONING ABROAD

To call home from Amsterdam, dial the international access code 00, followed by the code for the relevant country. Dialling codes are as follows UK +44; USA and Canada +1; Australia +61; New Zealand +64; Ireland +353; South Africa +27.

Post

There are plenty of post offices around the city. They are usually open 09.00–17.00 Mon–Fri, with some of the larger offices also open on Saturday mornings. The main post office is at Singel 250 and stays open until 20.00 Mon–Fri. You can buy stamps at post offices, shops or hotels. At the time of writing, sending a postcard cost €0.55 within Europe and €0.70 to elsewhere in the world.

ELECTRICITY

Voltage in Amsterdam and throughout the Netherlands is 220V, 50Hz, with plugs being the usual two round-pin continental type. If you need an adapter or a voltage transformer, buy one before leaving home because it will be hard to find one in Amsterdam.

TRAVELLERS WITH DISABILITIES

Amsterdam is not the easiest place to navigate for those with physical disabilities. It's a medieval city with many cobbled streets, narrow pathways and bridges, and the traffic of cars, pedestrians, trams and rapidly moving cyclists is busy. Lots of the buildings are old, narrow and on several floors, so check in advance before booking a hotel.

Metro stations are equipped with lifts, but these may not always be easy to find. Trams and buses are not equipped for wheelchair access; railway stations however generally are. There are special private wheelchair-accessible taxi services in the city such as **Garskamp** (📞 020 633 3943) and **Connexion Jonkcars** (📞 020 606 2200); advance booking is recommended. Those visitors with motorised wheelchairs can use the bike paths.

For a good source of travel-related information contact the **ANWB Disabled Department** on 📞 070 314 1420 🌐 www.anwb.nl

TOURIST INFORMATION

The Netherlands Tourist Board is known as the **Vereniging voor Vreemdelingenverkeer**, or **VVV** (🅦 www.vvv.nl). There are offices throughout the country, including several in Amsterdam. They are generally very good, with lots of free information and helpful staff who speak several languages. There is a small fee for booking accommodation or tickets.

There are VVV offices at Platform 2B of Centraal Station, next to Burger King, and on the main square immediately outside the station. Other offices are scattered across town. 📞 9099 400 4040 🅦 www.amsterdamtourist.nl

MORE USEFUL WEBSITES

www.amsterdamtourist.nl
www.aub.nl
www.visitamsterdam.com
www.holland.com

BACKGROUND READING

Geert Mak's Amsterdam: A Brief Life of the City by Geert Mak. It is anything but brief, though never less than fascinating.
The Diary of a Young Girl by Anne Frank. If you have read it already, read it again.
Outsider in Amsterdam by Janwillem van de Wetering. First in the excellent crime novel series entitled Amsterdam Cops.
The *Van der Valk* crime novels by Nicolas Freeling are set in Amsterdam.
The *Inspector Dekok* mysteries by A C Baantjer are also good, easy reads and very atmospheric.

🔺 *Canal in Amsterdam at night*

Emergencies

Toll-free number for all emergencies ● 112
Call from any phone box, landline or mobile phone. There are
English-speaking operators 24 hours a day.

MEDICAL SERVICES

For 24-hour emergency medical and dental help, call the **Central
Medical Service** ● 020 592 3434. English-speaking operators can
tell you which doctors and dentists are on duty, and which of them
speak English. Hotels and pharmacies can also advise.

There is a 24-hour accident and emergency department at the
Onze Lieve Vrouwe Gasthuis hospital ● 1e Oosterparkstraat 279
● 020 599 9111.

There are two types of chemist or pharmacy. For general
medical supplies and non-prescription drugs go to a *drogist* and
for prescription drugs take your prescription to the *apotheek*.
These are normally open 08.30–17.30 Mon–Fri. Information about
pharmacies open outside of normal hours is usually posted in
pharmacy windows and given in the daily newspaper, *Het Parool*.

POLICE

In case of theft or other emergency, the most convenient police
station for the city centre is near Leidseplein at ● Lijnbaansgracht 219

There are other stations at ● Prinsengracht 1109 and
● Beursstraat 33. The headquarters, the Hoofdbureau van Politie,
is on Elandsgracht. For general enquiries call ● 0900 8844

EMERGENCY PHRASES

Fire!	**Help!**	**Stop!**
Brand!	Hulp!	Stop!
Brant!	*Hul-ep!*	*Stop!*

Call the fire brigade!
Waarschuw de brandweer!
Vaarskoow de brant-veer!

Call the police!
Bel de politie!
Bel de pol-eet-see!

Call an ambulance!
Waarschuw een ziekenauto!
Vaarskoow an zeeken-owtoe!

EMBASSIES & CONSULATES

Australian Embassy ⓐ Carnegielaan 4, The Hague ⓣ 070 310 8200
British Consulate ⓐ Koningslaan 44, Amsterdam ⓣ 020 676 4343
Canadian Embassy ⓐ Sophialaan 7, The Hague ⓣ 070 311 1600
New Zealand Embassy ⓐ Carnegielaan 10, The Hague ⓣ 070 346 9324
South African Embassy ⓐ Wassenaarseweg 40, The Hague
ⓣ 070 392 4501
United States Consulate ⓐ Museumplein 19, Amsterdam
ⓣ 020 575 5309

INDEX

WHAT'S IN YOUR GUIDEBOOK?

Independent authors Impartial up-to-date information from our travel experts who meticulously source local knowledge.

Experience Thomas Cook's 165 years in the travel industry and guidebook publishing enriches every word with expertise you can trust.

Travel know-how Contributions by thousands of staff around the globe, each one living and breathing travel.

Editors Travel-publishing professionals, pulling everything together to craft a perfect blend of words, pictures, maps and design.

You, the traveller We deliver a practical, no-nonsense approach to information, geared to how you really use it.

Editorial/project management: Lisa Plumridge
Copy editor: Monica Guy
Layout/DTP: Pat Hinsley
Proofreader: Wendy Janes

The publishers would like to thank the following individuals and organisations for supplying their copyright photographs for this book: Ron Beekmeijer/SXC.hu, page 75; BigStockPhoto.com (Diego Cervo, page 59; Eric Gevaert, pages 146–7; Ivonne Wierink, pages 40–1); Eric Gevaert/Dreamstime.com, page 9; Jarno Gonzalez/Stockxpert.com, page 119; iStockphoto.com (Andrew Dawson, page 32; Jarno Gonzalez, page 37; Matthew Gordon, page 29; Arjan de Jager, page 7; Warwick Lister-Kaye, page 153; Michel de Nijs, page 5); G & A Scholiers/SXC.hu, page 39; Neil Setchfield, all others.

Send your thoughts to
books@thomascook.com

- **Found a great bar, club, shop or must-see sight that we don't feature?**
- **Like to tip us off about any information that needs a little updating?**
- **Want to tell us what you love about this handy little guidebook and more importantly how we can make it even handier?**

Then here's your chance to tell all! Send us ideas, discoveries and recommendations today and then look out for your valuable input in the next edition of this title.

Email the above address (stating the title) or write to: CitySpots Project Editor, Thomas Cook Publishing, PO Box 227, Coningsby Road, Peterborough PE3 8SB, UK.